PSILOCYBIN MUSHROOMS

The Ultimate Step-By-Step Guide to Cultivation and Safe Use of Psychedelic Mushrooms - Learn How to Grow Magic Mushrooms, Enjoy Their Benefits, and Manage Their Side-Effects

BY

CALVIN NEWMAN

TABLE OF CONTEN

INTRODUCTION _______________________________________ 5

PART I: WHY PSILOCYBIN MUSHROOMS? __________ 11

Chapter 1: The Nature of Psilocybin Mushrooms _____________ 13

Chapter 2: Therapeutic Benefits of Psilocybin _______________ 23

Chapter 3: Why Magic Mushrooms are Ideal for You ___________ 26

PART II: HOW TO GROW YOUR FAVORITE PSYLOCYBIN MUSHROOMS _______________________________________ 35

Chapter 4: Why You Need to Grow Your Own Psilocybin Mushrooms ____ 37

Chapter 5: Where to Grow Your Psychedelic Mushrooms ________ 40

Chapter 6: How to Grow Your Magic Mushrooms _____________ 45

PART III: HOW TO HARVEST, TREAT AND STORE YOUR PSILOCYBIN MUSHROOMS ____________________ 101

Chapter 7: How to Harvest Your Psilocybin Mushrooms ________ 103

Chapter 8: How to Cure and Store Your Psilocybin Mushrooms _ 109

PART IV: HOW TO CONSUME YOUR DELICIOUS PSILOCYBIN MUSHROOMS _______________________ 113

Chapter 9: Your Shroom Consumption Methods _____________ 115

Chapter 10: How to Take a Dose of Your Magic _______________ 124

Chapter 11: How to Savor Your Meal-time With Shroom Edibles Recipes ____ 142

PART V: HOW TO MAKE YOUR PSYLOCYBIN MUSHROOMS YOUR ETERNAL LIFESTYLE__________ 161

Chapter 12: How to Use Micro-dosing to Inspire Your Daily Experiences____ 164

Chapter 13: How to Recharge Your Life, Boost your joy, and Experience More Happiness through Psychedelic Lifestyle ______ 172

Chapter 14: How to Tap into the Psychedelic Power of Shrooms to Reset and Reprogram your Mindset _________________ 206

CONCLUSION _________________________________ 234

INTRODUCTION

Welcome to the world of psychedelics! Here we are.

You have probably heard of psilocybin mushrooms. If not, then, worry not. This book is about you and those who wish to learn more. Psychedelics? Psilocybin? Do not get scared by these two big terms. Behind them rests simple feelings. Psychedelics are those substances that, when you consume them, they take you into another world of imaginations. Psilocybin is just one of those psychedelic substances commonly found in mushrooms. Psilocybin is the marriage bond between mushrooms and psychedelics.

Not all mushrooms are psychedelic. Only a few species exist that nature chose to hide in them this potent magic. A potency that when consumed, brings new realities to the perception of the nature of things and the nature of beings. If you have never witnessed your mind concocting a new magnificent reality right before your sight, this experience can be a miracle. Yet, this is not new. The gods of our ancestors made them experience this long before we were born. It is our turn to pass over this magic to our future generations. This book is just about that – to let you experience this magical reality, and from that experience, you can narrate your experience to them as a first-hand witness.

Behind this new phenomenal reality, your mental reformation takes place - Stress disappears. Anxiety dies. Calmness settles. Your brainpower gets re-energized. Thus, it is not just the sensations that matter. No. Those are merely beautiful symptoms of some great mental transformations taking place behind the curtain of your conscious mind. It is a renewal. It is a rebirth - of the entire mind.

There are many psychedelics, but I have decided to bring psilocybin. Why psilocybin? There is a reason why I am recommending this potion. The nature of psilocybin makes it compelling. It has a host of therapeutic benefits to your health that you cannot afford to miss. Later in this book, I will unveil to you plenty of reasons as to why psilocybin is ideal for you.

Why not other psychedelics?

Yes, there is LSD. LSD is probably the most potent of all psychedelics. It is much more potent than the mushroom's psilocybin. However, it is synthetic – with not-so-pleasant side effects. It is not natural. Yet, its synthesis is such complex that it can only be done in the labs by qualified experts. What about psilocybin mushrooms? Well, our ancestors knew how to use them – as illiterate as they were. They did not need a lab. They did not need a technical degree. Nothing but the sheer taste of their tongue buds.

So, you don't need to be an expert to get the benefits of psilocybin found in the mushrooms. All you need is the knowledge of what these types of mushrooms are, where to find them, how to grow them right in your home, and how to consume them. It would be such complex to set an LSD lab in your home, and extremely risky.

Why not any other kind of mushrooms?

Nature knows how to be fair. There are mushrooms for life (food and healing); there are mushrooms for heaven (leisure and relaxation), and there are mushrooms for 'death' (toxic or poisonous). Yet, even within each category, some species are more potent in their respective category than others.

Why Psilocybin mushrooms? Psilocybin mushrooms are the mushrooms for heaven. They are the gods' secret potent. They are the ones endowed with the power to drive you to 'high' heavens. They are the only ones with the potency of this naturally-occurring psychedelic substance – psilocybin.

Are psilocybin mushrooms legal?

Laws are not static, but dynamic. Throughout history, there are many things which had been criminalized only to be legalized later due to their immense benefits to society. One such case is marijuana. Marijuana was once criminalized across the world. However, due to the overwhelming scientific discoveries of its immense medical benefits, many countries have now decriminalized its use for medicinal purposes. The same is the case with psilocybin mushrooms. The immense scientific evidence of the mental health benefits of psilocybin mushrooms has meant that many jurisdictions are now reversing the criminalization laws.

Not all countries move at the same pace of development. There will always be laggards. Thus, it is important to find out whether your country allows you to grow or consume psilocybin mushrooms or not before you take up the trip to this psychedelic world.

Can I have my own psilocybin mushrooms garden?

Yes, you can grow psilocybin mushrooms – right in your home. You do not need acreages of land. Just some little space in your spare room is enough. You can even use some space in your garage, balcony, or even verandah! All you need to ensure is that you create the right conditions for the mushrooms to grow, flourish, and pump in the psilocybin.

With a simple knowledge of how to grow container plants, you can easily grow your own psilocybin mushrooms and get that psychedelic potency right within your reach. You can experience the world of your ancestors and that of your future descendants - right in the present – psilocybin is the magic! No lab required. No complex expertise needed—only the magic mushrooms.

I am going to show you how to select the right materials and the right tools, how to prepare the right substrate, how to set the right temperature and light conditions. And, ultimately, how to tend to your budding mushrooms up to maturity.

How do I harvest, treat, and store my psilocybin mushrooms?

Apart from the growing environment, the potency of psilocybin depends heavily on how the mushroom is treated and stored after harvest. Furthermore, the extra benefits such as Vitamin D and other essential minerals are significantly enhanced through proper treatment and storage.

In this book, I will show you how to harvest, treat, and store your magic mushrooms so that you get the most optimal psychedelic effect, plus other health benefits.

What is the best way for me to consume my psychedelic mushrooms?

Just like other foods, having the best ingredients does not necessarily guarantee you a delicious meal. Bad cooks turning great ingredients into a horrible meal is almost a proverb. It takes a mastery of culinary arts to achieve a great meal. This is the reason why I have indulged myself in showing you how to consume your delicious psilocybin mushrooms. You will learn different methods of consuming your beloved mushrooms, how to derive the consumable extracts, and the different recipes you need to make you savor the magical taste while keeping monotony at bay.

This book is a delicacy in its regard. Keep sampling more. Tons of sumptuous knowledge beckons you to devour.

Can I have a life-long transforming experience with these magic mushrooms?

Sure! The magic part of psychedelic mushrooms is that you create and sustain a life-long experience out of consuming them. What you need is to have a daily micro-dose of psilocybin. This micro-dose is powerful enough to boost your mental acuity yet, light enough not to export you into another world permanently.

With the various methods of consumption and several recipes provided in this book, you can enjoy an endless magical lifestyle.

So, what next?

Dive deep into this world of psychedelics. Get started with the first Part, and more will keep flowing as you enjoy this highly sensual psychedelic immersion. Keep reading...

PART I: WHY PSILOCYBIN MUSHROOMS?

A forest of magic mushrooms. Image source: pxfuel.com

Overview

Those who are yet to experience the magic potency of psilocybin mushrooms are left wondering, "why psilocybin mushrooms?'

This is the big question that I am going to answer in this Part. While the answer could be as simple as having a bite of this magic mushroom, it is better to know in advance what to expect.

I am going to explain to you what makes this mushroom gain its magic powers, the kind of benefits it bestows to your health, and why it is ideal for you.

Topics covered

- The nature of psilocybin mushrooms

- Therapeutic benefits of psilocybin

- Why magic mushrooms are ideal for you

Chapter 1: The Nature of Psilocybin Mushrooms

The best way to know, understand, and appreciate psilocybin mushrooms is to master the details about their nature. First of all, you need to know their physical characteristics. This will help you distinguish them from other species. Secondly, you need to know their chemical composition, which is their common bond (psilocybin). Thirdly, you need to understand the chemical composition and pharmacological characteristics of psilocybin – the potent compound responsible for the magical effect. Lastly, you need to understand how psilocybin works to achieve this magical effect.

Physical characteristics of Psilocybin mushrooms

With almost 200 species of psilocybin mushrooms, it is hard to come to common physical characteristics. However, as a rule of thumb, we can outline some common features, even though they might not apply to all the psilocybes.

Identifying the magic mushrooms

With almost 200 species of psychedelic mushrooms out of thousands of mushroom species, it is a daunting task to distinguish between psychedelic and non-psychedelic mushrooms.

Nonetheless, two fundamental attributes (according to Stametsian Rule) can help us separate the magic from the non-magic. Psychedelic mushrooms have:

- Bruise blue flesh

- Gilled, with a purple-brown or black spore print

Apart from these general attributes, each species of psilocybe has a unique identity. With almost 200 species of psilocybes, we cannot afford to give specific identities of each in this book. Nonetheless, we have described the general attributes to look out for when choosing your preferred species of psilocybin mushroom for planting.

Parts of the magic mushrooms

Apart from features described under the Stametsian Rule, magic mushrooms are largely similar to other types of mushrooms in terms of their main parts.

The following diagram depicts the major parts of a psychedelic mushroom:

MUSHROOM ANATOMY

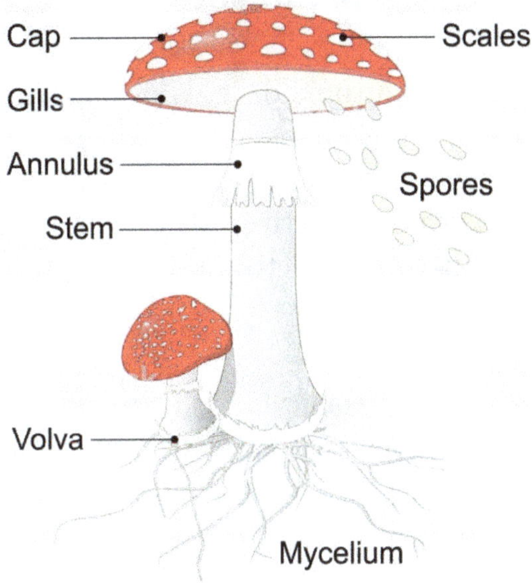

Parts of a magic mushroom. Image source: Istockphoto.com

Chemical composition of psilocybin

Psilocybin is a tryptamine alkaloid extracted from various types of fungi. When ingested, psilocybin is converted into pharmacologically active form psilocin. While psilocin also exists in psychedelic mushrooms, it is in trace quantities. Thus, the bulk of the psychedelic effect is derived from the converted psilocin rather than from the naturally occurring psilocin.

Pharmacological characteristics of psilocybin

Psilocybin is a psychotropic drug, which means that it is a drug that has a psychedelic effect. It is regarded as a psychedelic prodrug. A prodrug is a chemical compound that is pharmacologically inactive. However, after getting consumed, it becomes activated through the body's metabolism.

As a Type 1B prodrug, Psilocybin is activated intracellularly, that is, within the cell membrane. Typical cells affected by psilocybin include the liver cells, brain cells, mucosal GI cell, lung, among others.

The pharmacological evolution of psilocybin mushrooms

Psilocybin mushrooms evolved to adapt to its harsh conditions. Initially, this magic mushroom was just like other mushrooms – without psilocybin. However, due to the need to survive against ants and such other predators, the mushroom started to develop psilocybin chemicals as a defense mechanism.

The psilocybin chemical acted as a way of making the ants easily get satiated and thus eat less of the mushrooms. This ensures more mushrooms survive to maturity.

What psilocybin mushrooms share with LSD

There is no doubt that LSD is currently the most potent psychedelic drug. Thus, it can be considered a standard of measure when it comes to psychedelic effect. Any competitor must, therefore, measure up against it. Psilocybin is no exception.

What are the similarities between psilocybin and LSD?

Those who have never consumed magic mushrooms often wonder whether there is any similarity between psilocybin and LSD. This is probably because they would like to choose between the two. Mostly, it is consumers of LSD that are interested in knowing whether they can gain the same effect from magic mushrooms as an alternative.

Both psilocybin and LSD are:

- psychedelic substances – while there are differences in the kind of reactional behaviors that they cause to the consumer, both of them make the consumer feel 'high'.

- Fungal-based – both psilocybin and LSD are chemical compounds found in fungi. LSD is found in the Ergot fungus, a common parasitic fungus that attaches itself to the rye grain stalk.

- Not addictive – unlike marijuana and such other 'high' substances, neither psilocybin nor LSD is addictive. This means that you can consume them without the fear of becoming their unwilling slave entrapped in their 'high' snare. This allows you the freedom of choice and flexibility. Furthermore, should you find yourself in a situation or place where the magic mushroom is lacking, you won't get tormented by addictive craving that often accompanies hard drugs.

What makes psilocybin different from its LSD competitor

While there are similarities between psilocybin and LSD, there are striking differences that make it preferable to choose one over the other.

The following are the main differences:

- Psilocybin is a naturally-occurring substance while LSD is a synthetic substance

- While mushrooms are largely legal in most jurisdictions, LSD is illegal

- LSD acts instantly upon ingestion – right from the mouth. Psilocybin takes time to act after being ingested as it has to be converted into psilocin within the small intestines.

- LSD has no taste. Psilocybin has a disgusting taste

- The effect of LSD lasts for about 8 to 12 hours, while that of psilocybin lasts for between 6 and 8 hours.

- LSD liberates your individuality as it makes you experience internal happiness and joy. On the other hand, psilocybin brings spiritual connections between the individual and nature. This is why, unlike LSD, the magic mushroom is largely used in religious and ritualistic ceremonies.

- LSD has less of a hallucinating effect than psilocybin. While LSD increases mental focus and intensity on objects, thus bringing more clarity to their details, psilocybin distorts the clarity by virtually altering the image details such as color, shape, motion, etc. Thus, consumers of LSD won't experience static objects acquiring motion while consumers of psilocybin will more likely see stationary objects moving. Hence while LSD enhances the clarity of reality, psilocybin alters that reality.

How psilocybin works to achieve its phantastica

While ants get quickly satiated from eating psilocybin, humans get 'high' instead. How? This is because of the secondary compound that psilocybin is converted into – psilocin.

The conversion of psilocybin into psilocin

When you ingest psilocybin, it gets converted in the small intestines to psilocin. The psilocin gets transported into the brain through the bloodstream after absorption.

Psilocin mimics the brain's serotonin, a hormone responsible for the 'feel-good' effect.

How it affects the brain function

By mimicking serotonin, psilocin not only makes you 'feel good' but also distorts your perception and alters your thoughts and mood while maintaining your lucid awareness.

In a neurological sense, psilocin doesn't really 'mimic' serotonin but acts as its trigger.

The serotonin trigger

Psilocin acts as a brain receptor that triggers the release of serotonin from synaptic vesicles of neurons. Serotonin is a chemical responsible for the 'feel-good' effect. Thus, there is a change in mood, and you start feeling happier and more satisfied with life.

Low levels of serotonin are associated with negative moods, stress, anxiety, and even depression. By boosting serotonin levels, psilocin helps to relieve these symptoms and thus remedy these conditions.

The neural avalanche

You've probably seen or watched an avalanche taking place. It is a sudden massive movement of earth debris. Imagine the same happening with neurons! Yes, that's what happens when you start seeing the earn moving under your feet, objects changing colors, and transforming shapes, among other perceptive distortions that happen when the magic mushroom ferries you to the phantastica havens.

Behind this perceptive distortion, there is massive activation of the neurons. It is like a set of switches shutting one after another in rapid succession, thus creating a switch-on domino effect. This is what brings up a 'lighted moment' characterized by intense awareness. In this state, you begin to see things with much clarity that were hitherto hidden in the subconscious mind. Different 'dark rooms' of thoughts are 'lighted up' like an entire city being instantly lighted up such that sections that were previously invisible due to darkness instantly becomes visible.

In the brain's case, there is increased coordination and synchronization of the different functions of the brain, and the dark curtain that separates different sections of the brain seems to be suddenly broken such that the brain functions a one holistic system function towards one common end. This synergetic illumination increases the intensity of focus and the depth of concentration on that which is being perceived.

Chapter 2: Therapeutic Benefits of Psilocybin

Psychedelic mushrooms are distinguished for their therapeutic benefits. This is because they possess psilocybin.

They magically break your mental shackles, nurture your oneirogenic fantasies, and raise your entheogenic spirits, among other therapeutic benefits.

Breaking the mental shackles

Have you ever felt imprisoned in your mind? Have you ever felt that no matter how you try to free yourself from a certain set of thoughts or ways of thinking, you still find yourself trapped?

Our minds, like computers, operate based on a set program. This program, commonly referred to as the mindset, runs in a rather predetermined way. Thus, the only way to have a new way of thinking, a new kind of mental freedom, a new set of thoughts flowing is to reprogram your mindset.

Drawing from our computer analogy, however good a program is, if the CPU is limited, the program cannot achieve its optimal function. The CPU is nothing but a circuit of carefully wired logic gates. The same is the case with the brain. The brain circuitry, though much more complex, works similarly as the CPU. To radically alter the way this circuitry works, then it has to be rewired.

Hence, to break the mental shackles, there are two things you must do:

- Rewire the brain circuitry

- Reprogram your mindset

Psilocybin works on brain circuitry. It reconnects the disconnected parts. It creates newer and better connections that need to speed up certain functions.

Once this rewiring is done, your brain is supercharged. This way, it becomes easy for you to discover new opportunities to create better programs. This works the same way the computer world works. When a more powerful CPU is created, this creates an opportunity for more sophisticated software programs.

Nurturing your oneirogenic fantasies

Oneirogenic substances are those substances that 'create' dreams. Oneirogenic mushrooms enable you to enter the dream world while still in a state of consciousness. You can experience your lucid dreams intermingled with the real world to form a new reality.

The magnificence of this oneirogenic experience can be greatly appreciated when you are suffering from bad moods, depression, and such low moments. The magic mushrooms simply lift you beyond the clouds of depression and dampened spirit such that you can isolate yourself from the traps of negative experiences.

Soaring your spirit to its phantastica 'nirvana'

Nirvana is a Buddhist term for a world where there is no suffering. It is a world where selfish desire is overcome.

Psilocybin mushroom brings that sense of connectedness to the nature of beings and the nature of things. Just as it brings the connectedness of the various brain parts and functions, it also brings connectedness of the various social relationships.

More than anything else, it brings that connectedness between our physical realms and spiritual realms such that we feel them co-existing synergistically within the same domain.

The boundary between heaven and earth diminishes as our minds transcend these physical limitations.

Chapter 3: Why Magic Mushrooms are Ideal for You

Those who have taken a safe trip to the phantastica world of magics have never looked back. Not because they've become hopeless addicts, but because they've gained freedom unmatched elsewhere – the freedom to choose the best magic – and no choice has come close to a world in which the shroom's magic takes them.

You too can make a choice, a choice that you will never have to look back with regrets. It is a choice that you will be pleased to make every time and again.

Why? This is because magic mushrooms are ideal for you. We've already mentioned that they are non-addictive. Also, they are friendly to the brain, good for the moods, healthy to the body, and good for the appetite, among other great therapeutic benefits.

Let's explore these benefits, one-by-one...

They are non-addictive

The magic in the shrooms is one that liberates your mind. It is one that sets you free. It is not a magic that promises you heaven but takes you to an irreversible trip to hell. Those who repeatedly make this magic trip do so out of their own pleasant volition – not through compulsive addiction.

You can easily take a break from this joyous trip, disembark, and be earthly as you wait for the next trip. It is all your choice. It is all within your full uncompromised mental capacity.

They are good for your brain

These shrooms magically supercharge your brain. They magically boost your brain capacity. Yet, this is no miracle. It is neuroscience at work.

Like an expert electrician, the psilocin repairs damaged brain circuitry, and it activates shut logic gates (the neurons). And like a system engineer, it synchronizes the various brain subsystems, thus optimizing their synergy as a giant holistic system.

We've already seen how psilocin acts as a serotonin trigger that brings forth a neural avalanche. This is the mechanism that supercharges your brain, making it gain supernatural powers.

You can creatively tap into this supernatural brain power to boost your performance and productivity while enjoying your phantastica nirvana. This is why psychedelic mushroom is loved by the creative minds at Silicon Valley. You don't have to be a geek at the Silicon Valley to tap into the secret of this marvelous potential. This book makes it no longer a secret.

Their side effect is only temporary

There is no perfect medicine. Every medicine has its unpleasant side. Psilocin also has its rather unpleasant side effect. However, this side effect, like that of other medicines, varies from person to person. It also varies from dose to dose.

Some experience nightmares instead of dreams on their trip. What the magic mushroom does is to magnify your mental imagery and accentuate the details. Thus, if your mind is packed up with negative images, trashes of negative experiences, and uncluttered remnants of a traumatic past, this is likely going to play on your mental reel like a movie. Scary! But, blending psilomagic with NLP, you can reprogram the meaning of these mental images so that, instead of them being scary, they become entertaining. You can also use NLP to detach these mental images from your mindset.

However, some experience an endless dose of sweet dreams on their trip. This is because they have a good pack of positive mental images, a great memory of past experiences, and positive future visions. This also plays on your mental reel like a movie. Sweet!

So, what you require to do is to declutter your mind. Get rid of those negative mental images. And discard the unwanted baggage so that your trip can be lighter, and thus you can soar higher to your phantastica nirvana.

Using techniques such as NLP, neuroplasticity, mindfulness meditation, creative visualization, positive thinking, and positive affirmation can be of great help. The good thing is that you can use these techniques to set the kind of experience you want to encounter on your magical trip.

The best of everything is that – everything has an end. Whether it is, pleasure or pain, it will be temporary. Thus, the side effects will also be temporary. This grants you unlimited opportunity to keep on fine-tuning your journey every other time you make the trip.

They bring 'feel good' effect

Being a serotonin trigger, psilocybin mushrooms makes you feel happy, peaceful, and endowed with inner joy.

Why is serotonin such important?

To understand the important role that psilocybin plays by triggering serotonin, let's digest the important role played by serotonin itself.

Serotonin performs very important functions in the body. These include:

- Mood regulation – this is by far the most known function of serotonin.

- Bowel movement regulation – serotonin regulates bowel movement and other functions. It is also responsible for regulating appetite thus reducing your urge to over-eat

- Nausea – serotonin is responsible for creating nausea. Most people would feel disgusted by this. However, feeling nauseating is a very important mechanism as it helps you expel toxins from the gut, thus saving your life. It can also work in a preventive way by stopping you from further consumption of toxic substances.

- Clotting – serotonin is released by blood platelets when you are wounded to increase blood clotting. Clotting reduces bleeding, which saves a life.

- Sexual regulation – just as serotonin reduces your appetite when you are full, it also reduces your libido to limit the sexual urge from becoming overwhelming.

- Sleep-wake cycle – serotonin plays an important role in regulating your sleep-wake cycle (circadian rhythm). This helps you have regular and stable sleep patterns.

Risks associated with low serotonin levels include:

- Low moods and behavioral compulsions

- Poor memory

- Anxiety and worries

- Aggression

- Low self-esteem

- Disturbed sleep patterns and insomnia

- Mental obsessions

- Panics and phobias

- Obesity and eating disorders

- Irritable bowel

- Chronic pain and migraines

- Drug abuse – especially alcohol

Looking at the risks associated with low serotonin levels, you can greatly appreciate the role psilocybin plays in mitigating them by simply boosting the serotonin levels.

They are natural

Magic mushrooms are naturally-occurring ingredients. Their psilocybin is a naturally-occurring substance. Thus, unlike LSD, psilocybin is not artificially synthesized.

Being naturally-occurring means that they are less susceptible to the risk of artificial additives or reagents during the synthesizing process.

They are inexpensive

While the shelf price of LSD could be significantly lower due to pharmaceutical economies of scale, factoring the required capital outlay, the skills cost, and such other overhead costs, LSD cost is significantly higher than that of mushroom production.

Due to this low capital outlay, anyone with knowledge and keen interest such as you can be able to produce your mushroom. With this book, you have already acquired the knowledge - what awaits you is a keen interest, and you are ready to become a 'magic entrepreneur'.

They are therapeutic

What distinguishes psilocybin mushrooms from other edible mushrooms is its therapeutic benefits.

We have already seen how psilocin acts as a serotonin trigger. We have also seen the immense benefits of triggering serotonin.

Through this triggering mechanism, your moods are reset, your anxiety is wiped off, and your mental acuity is sharpened.

You are no longer depressed, no longer dull, but joyful and happy.

Thus, the magic mushroom is the safest vessel that can easily ferry you on that therapeutic trip to the euphoric world.

They are nutritional!

A lot of emphases is placed on the magic behind the psychedelic mushrooms, such that many people are dissuaded from remembering the nutritional benefits of these mushrooms.

The magic in psychedelic mushrooms does not steal away their nutritional value. Magic mushrooms are just as nutritional as any other mushroom, if not more.

Surprising nutritional facts:

- Cholesterol-free

- Fat-free

- Sodium-free

- Low-calorie

They are the best source of non-animal vitamin D. In fact, they continue accumulating vitamin D the more they are exposed to Sunlight during drying – probably the best reason why you should sun-dry them.

They are a rich source of minerals:

- Iron

- copper

- Potassium

- Phosphorous

- Selenium

Although nutritional content varies from species to species and the growth environment, generally, mushrooms possess the following nutritional content (per cup, or 70g):

- Protein: 2.2g

- Carbohydrates: 2.3g

- Calories: 15

- Sugars: 1.4g

- Fiber: 0.7g

As you can see, with magic shrooms, your trip to the mystic world is powered by a healthy dose of vitality.

PART II: HOW TO GROW YOUR FAVORITE PSYLOCYBIN MUSHROOMS

Psychedelic mushrooms marooning a tree trunk.

Image source: libreshot.com

Overview

There is nothing that raises your passion for gardening than the memorable moments of euphoric trips you make to the phantastica world.

The best way to keep living these trip experiences is to have a steady supply of magic shrooms. Markets can fail. The only surety that you have against market failures is to grow your shrooms close to your hood.

In this Part, I am going to show you how to grow your favorite psilocybin mushrooms so that you are guaranteed of optimal yield in the most efficient way using tools and materials within your reach.

Topics covered

- **Why** you need to grow your own psilocybin mushrooms

- **Where** to grow your psychedelic mushrooms

- **How** to grow your magic mushrooms

Chapter 4: Why You Need to Grow Your Own Psilocybin Mushrooms

Many regular users of magic mushrooms prefer to grow it rather than become dependent on the market supply that is prone to failure.

Some of the factors that such users consider include risks of international trade, quality considerations, and boosting essential gardening skills through a hobby.

Let's explore each of these factors, and they make it imperative for you to keep your magic garden.

To overcome the risks of international trade

Imports are more susceptible to trade wars, hot wars, tariffs, bans, and international politics. This means that you can easily find that your favorite magic is no longer available.

To avoid this potential scarcity plus other costs and inconveniences, it is necessary for you to grow your magic to ensure continued supply without running the risks of geopolitical disruptions.

To ensure that you have an adequate supply

Even if the source of your magic is not sourced internationally, local supplies can also get disrupted. Growing your magic does not necessarily mean that you will be immune to supply shocks and shortages, but you will have diversified sourcing options, thus reducing the risks.

To ensure that you are in control of its natural growth process

In most places, psychedelic mushrooms are imported. This means that they have taken ages to arrive at your convenience store.

Furthermore, they are likely going to have nutritional and therapeutic compromises. This is especially if you like taking them fresh.

Imported mushrooms are heavily mechanized and a lot often, are grown unnaturally. This compromises the potency of their magic plus their nutritional value. Furthermore, the storage and transport facilities could be contaminated, especially by heavy metals, thus increasing your risk of a toxic ingestion.

The best way to make sure that their nutritional value is guaranteed plus their magic potency remains undiluted. You have to be in control of their growth process.

To keep yourself busy and occupied with your shroom hobby

There no environmental activity that is as therapeutic as gardening. With gardening, you not only engage in physical activity but also relieve yourself from mental stress and potential depression. Even before the magic matures enough to work on your brain, the activity itself has already started working on it.

A hobby that helps you take care of nature, improve your nutrition, and reduce hunger is such a noble hobby. Your shroom garden is not just a garden but a spiritual sanctuary. Tend to this mycological garden, and you will find your energy flow being harmoniously synchronized with that of nature.

Chapter 5: Where to Grow Your Psychedelic Mushrooms

The biggest question that faces urban dwellers is where to grow their magic mushrooms.

With the developed world comprising of almost 80% urban dwellers, it happens that most shroom consumers are urban dwellers. Yet, it is them that need to guarantee themselves of consistent supply, therapeutic potency, and nutritional value from their beloved magic.

Surprisingly, there is plenty of space within the urban dwellings where the magic mushrooms can easily grow and flourish.

I am not inventing a new space within your habitat but simply reminding you to look around and see it. There is enough space to grow your magic indoors... and, for some of you, there is still some space to grow your shrooms outdoors.

Growing magic indoors

Growing psychedelic mushrooms indoors is the most popular way for urban dwellers, maybe because people don't have enough space outdoors. Or, maybe because they want to keep privacy from prying eyes – especially, in grey-area jurisdictions where the magic is criminalized or simply not acceptable.

Nonetheless, whichever the case, and for whatever reason you may have, let's explore indoor spaces where you can puff in your magic.

Free room

If you have a small free room, this could be the best option. This is because, apart from controlling the light, you can also easily control the temperature and access. You can also be able to control the overall humidity.

A free room also allows you maximum creativity as to whether you want to have shelves, grounded bags, or even hanging bags for growing your shrooms.

Corridor & Verandah

If you have no free or suitable room, you can take advantage of the corridor or veranda. However, if you have no strict control over the access to the corridor/veranda, then you will need to have a cupboard-like or shelf enclosure so that other people have no direct access to your shrooms.

Balcony

A balcony is an ideal place, especially if it is exclusive to your house. Thus, you can control the movement in and out of the balcony. Furthermore, you can easily and partially enclose a part of the balcony so that it becomes like a small room. In case you don't want to enclose partially, you can still use the balcony just as you would do with the corridor and verandah.

Attic/loft

Attic/Loft is a great place to grow your shrooms. The loft is a room within the attic. Instead of using the entire attic (the space below the roof), you can partition it into lofts. This way, you can have a grow room, a materials/tools room, and even your restroom after hard work.

Garage

If you have a big garage space that is rarely used, you can make a small enclosure out of it and use it as a planting site for your shrooms.

Growing your magic shrooms outdoors

Growing mushrooms outdoor is not the recommended way as you have limited control over the growing conditions. Mushrooms grown outdoors tend to take longer to mature.

Since you have limited control over their growth condition, you cannot afford to accelerate their growth rate as you would do with indoor mushrooms.

Also, their productivity is often lower as the mushroom becomes more susceptible to the vagaries of weather.

However, if you have no indoor space, then, this remains the only option left. Some of the outdoor places where you can grow your shroom include the kitchen garden, grass shade, tree trunk, fence canopy, valley cave, among others.

Kitchen garden

The kitchen garden can be a nice place to plant your shrooms. The advantage of a kitchen garden is that you can use the kitchen garden to prepare compost for your shrooms as well as partition a small space to plant the shrooms.

Grass shade

Like a car shade, you can create a shade made of grass. The purpose of the grass is to prevent strong light and also create a damp environment where you can grow your shrooms. Grass can also act as a medium through which you can humidify the mushroom growing space.

Tree trunk

A rotting tree trunk is ideal for certain species of psilocybin mushrooms. Also, only certain trees can provide the substrate medium. Thus, while this can work, it is pretty challenging and requires first-hand knowledge of the tree species for the substrate and the mushroom species for the growth. Furthermore, the tree trunk is less ideal in urban setup than in rural setup.

Fence canopy

Certain hedge fences can easily provide a canopy plus humus that promotes the growth of fungi. You need to know the kind of trees/shrubs that can provide the required canopy and humus.

Valley cave

If you reside in a place that has rugged terrain, then, you can easily find some cave in a valley. This is an ideal place to plant those shroom species that easily grow in partially enclosed underground. If there is no cave, you can easily dig one for this purpose.

However, this is ideal in a rural setup as it is hard to find such terrain or such a space in an urban setup.

Chapter 6: How to Grow Your Magic Mushrooms

Now that you have decided where to grow your shrooms, the next thing is to know how to grow them in your chosen place.

The first thing to do is to decide on what is going to be your planting material. Once you choose your preferred planting material, you can then be able to determine the kind of substrate that is ideal for your planting material.

Having chosen the right substrate for your material, you can go ahead and prepare it. The substrate will require to be held in a container for planting. Container that holds the substrate should be ideal for your chosen planting site.

But before you embark on growing your mushroom, you must understand the entire lifecycle of your mushroom so that you can be able to tell with certainty at what stage of growth your mushroom is experiencing.

Understand the mushroom lifecycle

Understanding the mushroom lifecycle makes you get prepared for your mushroom's next stage of growth.

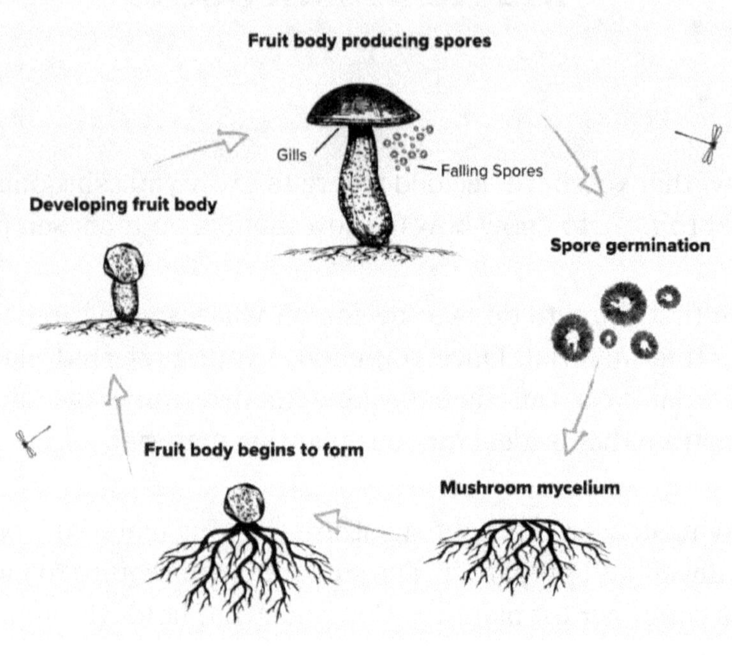

The mushroom lifecycle - Image source: nicepng.com

Without going into the seed-and-fruit-question as to what came first, let's avoid this controversy by beginning with the fruit (fruit body) as depicted in the above diagram.

The cap (fruit body) has gills beneath it. The gills, when mature, are populated with **spores** just as pollen grains in a petal. These pores appear as brownish micro-granules. The pattern they form on the gills is called **spore print**.

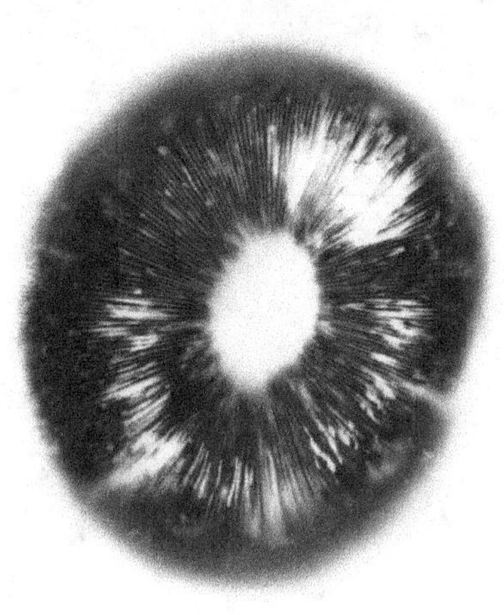

Spore prints.

After a while, the spores start falling on the ground. If you use a magnifying lens, you can easily observe them on the ground when fallen. If you want to prepare your own culture, before the gills open up, you place on the ground tinfoil that not only covers the cap's circumference but extends some few centimeters beyond just to capture those spores dispersed farther by the wind.

Spores on a glass slate observed through a magnifying lens

The spores germinate **hyphae**. A hypha is just like a bud on a germinating seed. However, unlike buds, they are simply sexually-active organs. Compatible hyphae mate to form fertilized **mycelium**. Mycelium appears as a white root-like network of fiber.

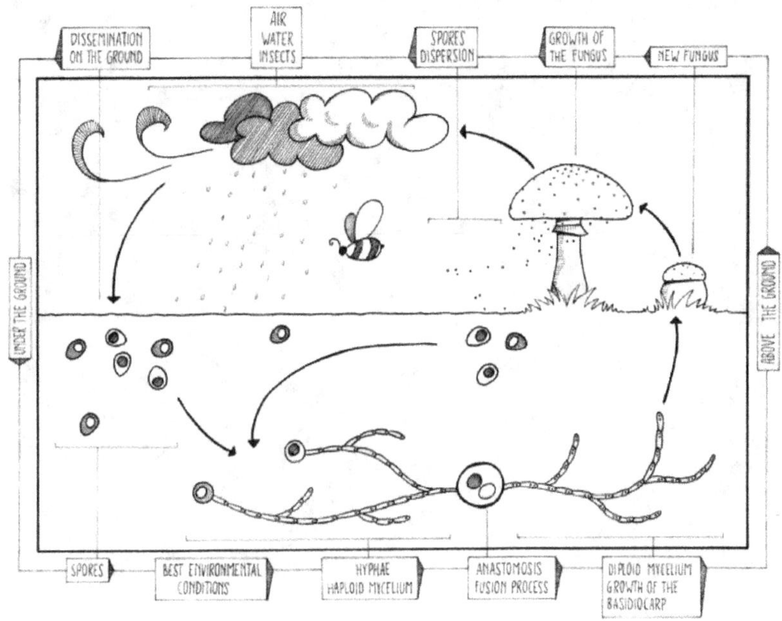

Mushroom sexual reproduction lifecycle (from spores to mycelium)

Mycelium expands to form a **mycelium colony** on the substrate. This expansion is what we call colonization, and it occurs during the incubation period (3-4 weeks, in a controlled environment).

Hyphae on the ground – early stages of expansion

On the surface, the mycelium colony can appear as white meshed threads holding the surface. These threads can sew together lumps of debris. However, the threads are too weak to resist the braking force of your hand.

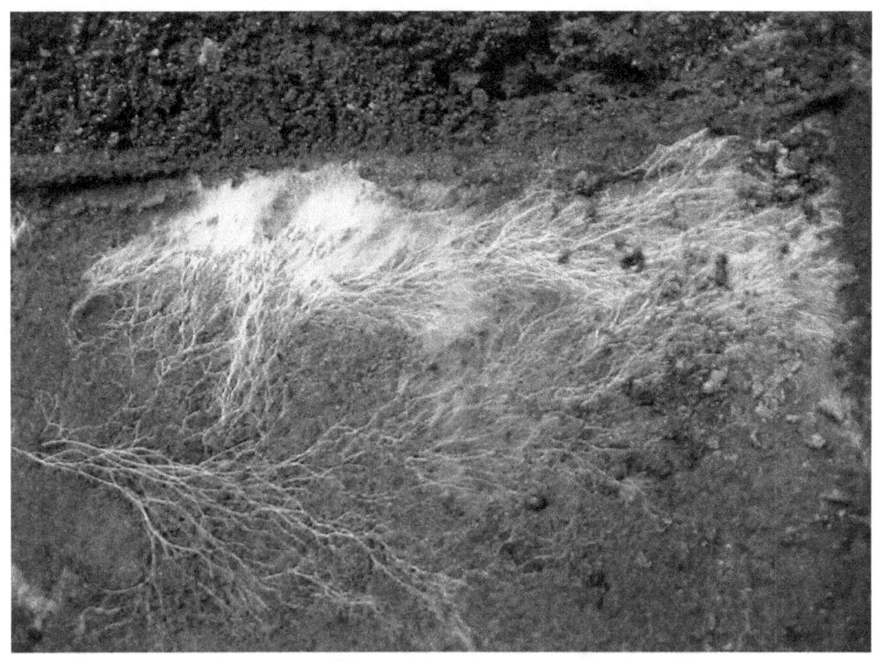

A fully-formed Mycelium colony

After colonization, mycelium condenses into **hyphal knots**. Hyphal knots are tiny growth lumps. The **hyphal knot** develops into **primordia**.

A primordium is a baby mushroom. It appears as a pin-like formation, which eventually protrudes to form the mushroom cap.

Mushroom primordia

To honor Charles Darwin's theory of survival for the fittest, natural selection occurs such that only the fittest primordium in a cluster is left to continue growing while those that are not fit or have low chances of survival are left to die. Eventually, the dead become humus for the surviving ones.

The fittest primordium gets enough space and nutrients to grow into a fruiting body. After a short while, the fruiting matures into a full mushroom ready for heavens (harvest!). To the Psilonauts, this fully-grown blossom is nature's beckoning call to transcendent heavens. The ecstatic expectancy is filled with pregnant fantasies of psilonautic trips to the worlds beyond.

Well, we are still here in the garden. To complete the lifecycle, the proudly brave mushroom stands out fully occupying its domain. If you've got to pick, just do it tenderly. Don't brutalize its pride. And just pick enough for your trip. If there is more to share, do share with others. You can also become a shroompreneur (shrooms entrepreneur) by selling them for profit.

A fully-grown **Amanita muscaria** standing tall

Out of the dream into reality, let's go planting...

Decide on your preferred planting material

To get the right planting material, you have to decide on the mushroom species that you want to get its magic from.

There are two options when it comes to planting material:

- Spores

- Spawns

You can use spores if you are more experienced with growing mushrooms and you can easily access mature mushrooms whereby you can be able to tap their falling spores.

However, if you are a newbie, the best option is to use spawns which come in the form of grow-kits.

The grow-kits have a ready-made culture. This culture comprises a substrate that is already colonized by mycelium and thus all you need is to break the substrate into pieces that you can use to inoculate the secondary substrate.

The various species of psilocybin mushrooms to choose from

There are almost 200 species of psilocybes. Thus, it would be daunting to list and describe all of them in this book. Nonetheless, we are going to consider the most common types of psilocybes.

The following are the top (7) species of psilocybes that you can consider:

1. *Psilocybe cubensis (Stropharia cubensis)*

Psilocybe cubensis is probably the most common of all psilocybe species. It is found in most tropical lands – from Asia to Africa and the Americas.

main features

Cap (pileus):

- Shape – conic (pagoda-shaped) while young. Flat or convex while aged.

- Color – reddish-cinnamon when young and golden-brown when aged.

- Width - 2-9cm

- Texture – smooth. Slimy when moist.

Gills (Lamella):

- Color – whitish at first. Turns purple-grey upon maturity and then black as it ages.

- Veil – deep purple

- Spore print – dark-brown or purple

Stipe (Stem/stalk):

- Color – white-yellowish. Manifests blue hue when bruised or aged.

- Length – 4-15cm

- Thickness – 4-14mm

- Ring (annulus) – white ring

Spores (when deposited):

- Color – brown to dark purple.

- Shape – elongated ellipsoid

- Size - 11.5–17 x 8–11 micrometers

Potency:

- Psilocybin – 0.63%

- Psilocin – 0.60%

- Baeocystin – 0.025%

Strains:

- Golden teacher
- Huautla
- Penis Envy
- Blue Meanie
- B+ Cubensis
- PF Classic
- Z Strain
- Orissa India
- Cambodian
- Alacabenzi
- Florida White (F+)
- Many more...

Habitat:

- Substrate - highly versatile and adaptable. However, straw, Brown Rice Flower (BRF), Psilocybe Fanaticus Technique (PF-Tek), rye grain, and manure are commonly used for psilocybe cubensis cultivation.

- Location – tropics and sub-tropics

The most distinct feature(s):

- Thick, dense stems

- Large, broad caps

Psilocybe cubensis

Psilocybe cubensis is highly versatile and can adapt to different climatic conditions and substrates. This makes it ideal for beginners and is often their first choice.

2. Psilocybe cyanescens

Known for its distinct wavy cap, psilocybe cyanescens is a native of North America. It has one of the highest levels of potency, as it contains about 0.85% psilocybin.

main features

Cap (pileus):

- Shape – rounded and closed around the stem while young. Broadly opens up to a convex shape when adult.

- Color – chestnut brown to caramel when young (or fresh). Yellowish-brown when aged (or dry)

- Width - 1.5–5 cm

- Texture – smooth. Slimy when moist.

- Umbo – the remains in place even as the cap turns convex. It becomes depressed with wavy margins upon maturity.

Gills (Lamella):

- Color – pale tan at the start. cinnamon-smoky brown upon full maturity.

- Spore print – dark-brown or purple

Stipe (Stem/stalk):

- Color – whitish. Manifests blue hue when bruised or aged.

- Length – 2-8cm

- Thickness – 2-5mm

- Ring (annulus) –

- Volva – silky. Covered with rhizomorphs (white mycelial tufts)

- Shape – slightly curved. Thicker towards the base.

Spores (when deposited):

- Color – brown to dark purple.

- Shape – elongated ellipsoid

- Size - 9-12 x 5-8 micrometers

Potency:

- Psilocybin – 0.85%

- Psilocin – 0.36%

- Baeocystin – 0.03%

Strains:

- N/A

Habitat:

- Substrate - decaying wood matter.

- Location – North America

The most distinct feature(s):

- Wavy cap

- Undulating edges

Psilocybe cyanescens

3. *Psilocybe stuntzii*

Nicknamed Stuntz's Blue legs and Blue Ringers, Psilocybe stuntzii is a rare species of magic mushrooms.

This mushroom has a characteristic sticky, brownish cap with brownish gills and brownish, ringed stalk.

main features

Cap (pileus):

- Shape – rounded and closed around the stem while young. Broadly opens up to a convex shape when adult. Slightly wavy and uplifted when adult.

- Color – dark to yellow-brown. Green-tinged on the margins

- Width - 1.5 - 4 cm

- Texture – smooth. Sticky when moist.

- Umbo – the remains in place even as the cap turns convex.

Gills (Lamella):

- Color – whitish at first. Turns purple-grey upon maturity and then black as it ages.

- Veil – bluish veil

- Spore print – dark-brown or purple

Stipe (Stem/stalk):

- Color – Yellowish

- Length – 3-6 cm

- Thickness – 3mm

- Ring (annulus) – membranous ring

- Volva – smooth to fibrous

- Shape – Thicker towards the base.

Spores (when deposited):

- Color – brown to dark purple.

- Shape – elongated ellipsoid. Pore at the tip

- Size - 8-12.5 X 6-8 micrometers

Potency(%):

- Psilocybin – 0.36%

- Psilocin – 0.12%

- Baeocystin – 0.02%

Habitat:

- Substrate – coniferous wood-chip mulch

- Location – Pacific North-West

The most distinct feature(s):

- Sticky cap

- Ringed stalk

Psilocybe stuntzii

4. *Psilocybe azurescens*

Fondly referred to as 'flying saucer' due to the shape of its cap once fully mature, psilocybe azurescens is the most potent of the known psilocybes.

A native of Oregon and Washington States in the US, psilocybe is very popular with outdoor growers.

main features

Cap (pileus):

- Shape – conic while young. Flat or convex while aged.

- Color – ochraceous brown. Pitted with dark blue or bluish-black zones when aged.

- Width - 3-10cm

- Texture – smooth. Viscous when moist.

- Umbo – nipple-like. Remains in place even as the cap turns convex or flat.

- Pellicle – colorless.

Gills (Lamella):

- Color – brownish

- Veil – bluish

- Spore print –purple-brown

Stipe (Stem/stalk):

- Color – silky white. Turns dingy-brown when aged.

- Length – 9-20cm

- Thickness – 3-6mm

- Ring (annulus) – bluish

- Volva – dingy-brown. Covered with rhizomorphs (white mycelial tufts)

- Shape – slightly curved. Thicker towards the base.

Spores (when deposited):

- Color – brown to dark purple.

- Shape – elongated ellipsoid

- Size - 11.5–17 x 8–11 micrometers

Potency:

- Psilocybin – 1.78%

- Psilocin – 0.38%

- Baeocystin – 0.35%

Strains:

- N/A

Habitat:

- Substrate - decaying wood matter, cow mulch, grass with high lignin content.

- Location – Oregon and Washington States in the US

The most distinct feature(s):

- 'Flying-saucer' cap

- Highest potency level.

- Outdoor cultivation

Psilocybe azurescens

5. *Psilocybe Mexicana*

Popularly known as 'the flesh of gods', Psilocybe Mexicana is aboriginal species of South America. It was traditionally used by the Aztech people for religious and spiritual purposes, thus deriving its nickname 'the flesh of gods'. Mexico is believed to be its ancestral home. However, it has extended its tentacles into Guatemala and Costa Rica.

main features

Cap (pileus):

- Shape – conic at the start. Convex at maturity

- Color –brown to ocherous when young. Beige to straw when aged.

- Width – 0.5–3 cm

- Texture – smooth. Viscid when moist.

- Umbo – small size

Gills (Lamella):

- Color – grey to purple-brown. Whitish edges.

- Veil – thinly fibrillose

- Spore print – dark purple-brown

Stipe (Stem/stalk):

- Color – Yellowish to brownish. Darkens with age.

- Length – 4-10cm

- Thickness – 1-3mm

- Ring (annulus) – reddish-brown flesh

- Volva – silky. Covered with rhizomorphs (white mycelial tufts)

- Shape – Uniform thickness, or narrower towards the base.

Spores (when deposited):

- Color – dark purplish brown

- Shape – ellipsoid (side view) and subrhomboid (face view)

- Size – 8-9.9 x 5.5-7.7 micrometers

Potency:

- Psilocybin – 0.25%

- Psilocin – 0.15%

- Baeocystin – 0.02%

Strains:

- N/A

Habitat:

- Substrate - grassy areas bordering deciduous forests, meadows, horse pastures.

- Location – Mexico, Guatemala, and Costa Rica

The most distinct feature(s):

- The stem is uniformly thick or slightly slender towards the base.

- Very small umbo

Psilocybe Mexicana

Psilocybe Mexicana is known for its truffles or sclerotia. If you are a fan of munching mushroom truffles, then the flesh of gods is a must-have in your mycological sanctuary.

6. *Psilocybe semilanceata*

Fondly known as 'Liberty cap' is one of the most liberally available psychedelic mushroom species. Despite its small size, Liberty cap is highly potent and can quicks send you packing on a trip to the mystic world.

main features

Cap (pileus):

- Shape – conic to obtusely conic. Rolled inwards while young. Unrolls outwards as it matures and even sometimes flattens or curls upwards.

- Color – dark chestnut brown when young (or fresh). Yellowish-brown when aged (or dry)

- Width - 0.5–2.5 cm

- Texture – smooth. Slimy when moist.

- Umbo – nipple-shaped

- Pellicle – viscid moist

Gills (Lamella):

- Color – brown at the start. Grey and then purplish-brown upon full maturity.

- Veil – cobweb-like partial veil

- Spore print – deep reddish purple-brown

Stipe (Stem/stalk):

- Color – Yellowish-brown

- Length – 4.5-14cm

- Thickness – 1-3.5mm

- Ring (annulus) – faded annular zone marks.

- Shape – flexuous and pliant. Thicker towards the base.

Spores (when deposited):

- Color – brown to dark purple.

- Shape –ellipsoidal

- Texture - smooth

- Size - 11-14 x 7-19 microns

Potency:

- Psilocybin – 0.98%

- Psilocin – 0.02%

- Baeocystin – 0.36%

Strains:

- N/A

Habitat:

- Substrate – sheep or cow dung, sedges (decaying root remains), highly organic wetlands

- Location – New Zealand, some parts of Europe (especially UK), Pacific North West.

The most distinct feature(s):

- Spear-shaped

- Rolled cap edges

Psilocybe semilanceata

Liberty cap does not shy away from growing liberally in the open fields, especially manured pasture. This is why it is generously available to psilonauts in many places in the world.

The distinctive feature of psilocybe semilanceata is its bell-shaped or conical shaped cap that is embellished with a nipple-like protrusion at its apex.

7. *Psilocybe baeocystis*

Known by the fond name of 'bluebells', psilocybe baeocystis has other names such as knobby tops, bottle caps, and olive caps. All these names describe the physical characteristics of the cap.

main features

Cap (pileus):

- Shape – conic to obtusely conic. Cap margins distinctly rippled and turned inwards.

- Color – dark olive-brown. Sometimes steel blue. Copper-brown towards the center when dried.

- Width - 1.5–5.5 cm

- Texture – smooth. Viscid when moist.

- Umbo – the remains in place even as the cap turns convex. It becomes depressed with wavy margins upon maturity.

- Pellicle – separable and gelatinous.

Gills (Lamella):

- Color – greyish or cinnamon brown with pallid edges

- Veil – evanescent partial veil

- Spore print – dark purplish-brown

Stipe (Stem/stalk):

- Color – pallid to brownish with a whitish filament. Yellowish towards the top

- Length – 5-7cm

- Thickness – 2-3mm

- Ring (annulus) – indistinguishable.

- Volva –Covered with rhizomorphs

- Shape – slightly curved. Thicker towards the base.

- Sturdiness - brittle

Spores (when deposited):

- Color –dark purplish-brown.

- Shape – ellipsoid (mango-like shape)

- Size - 9.5–13.7 x 5.5–6.6 micrometers

Potency:

- Psilocybin – 0.85%

- Psilocin – 0.59%

- Baeocystin – 0.01%

Strains:

- N/A

Habitat:

- Substrate - decaying wood matter (conifer mulch, wood chip, ground bark), peat moss, lawns, and pasture.

- Location – North America

The most distinct feature(s):

- Rippled edges

- Highly potent when fresh. Diminished potency when dry.

Psilocybe baeocystis

One unique feature of psilocybe baeocystiss that its potency is high when fresh and rapidly declines as it dries. Thus, this is a species that you have to munch while still fresh.

Factors determining your choice of psychedelic mushroom

1. *Availability of the planting material*

The availability of planting material is very important. You may wish to plant a certain species, but if it is not available in shops within your reach, then, it will be difficult for you to be assured of the materials when you need them most.

The first task to do is to take an inventory of magic species available within your locality. In case there is a certain species that you want to grow but is not available within your locality, check whether you can order it online and the reliability of doing so.

2. *The potency of the species*

Different species of psychedelic mushrooms are endowed with different levels of psilocybin potency. Genetically, some are more potent than others.

3. *The survival versatility of the species*

If you are a beginner, you would like to improve the chances of your project coming to fruition. Thus, you would prefer a species that has a higher survival versatility – that is, it can easily survive under different environments and more constrained conditions.

Some species are extremely sensitive and less versatile. These are not for you if you are a beginner.

4. *Your taste and preferences*

Just like food mushrooms, magic mushrooms have different tastes. The best way to grow your preferred taste is to sample tastes of various species and find out the taste that you like.

You will be more motivated to cultivate that magic that pleasantly scintillates your taste buds than the one that scares them away. Nonetheless, you have to balance between taste and potency. Some species are tastier but less potent while others are more potent but bitter.

5. *Your growth environment*

What environment are you capable of providing for your shrooms? Different species have a unique environment that they flourish.

In consideration of the previous factors, go for a species which you can easily create a conducive environment for its growth, flourish, and fruition.

6. *Your experience*

Your experience matters. You can either be an experienced grower or consumer - or both.

If you are a very experienced grower, then, you easily manage the growth of most species of magic mushrooms. However, if you are less experienced, especially a beginner, then, you will go for a species that is less demanding in terms of growth and nurturing.

As an experienced consumer, you will grow species that have high potency for your consumption. However, if you are new to the consumption of psychedelic mushrooms, then, you are better off starting with less potent mushrooms that won't give you a difficult time consuming them. This is safe for your test-drive.

After successful test-drive, you can gradually shift gear to growing more potent mushrooms as you gain experience of handling more rugged terrains on your trips.

Prepare the substrate

The substrate is the medium that provides nutrients, water, and support to the mycelium during the formative stages of the shroom and continues to provide a foundation for the growth to maturity of the shroom.

Without the substrate, the mushroom will simply not grow. Thus, the substrate has a huge impact on the survivability, growth, and productivity of the shrooms. This is why you have to select the right substrate material and prepare it well.

Selecting the right substrate material

There are many substrate materials to choose from. Factors that will determine your substrate material are:

1. Quality

Quality of the substrate material is important when it comes to survivability and growth of your shrooms. Qualitative factors include permeability, hydration, and aeration.

Permeability refers to the ability of the material to allow moisture to move within its membrane.

Hydration refers to the ability of the material to absorb and keep moisture. Mushrooms require a lot of moisture to grow and flourish.

Aeration refers to the ability of the material to easily allow air to circulate. A material with poor aeration will easily cause decay of the mycelium instead of growth.

The substrate material should be permeable, allows high levels of hydration and fairly aerated.

2. Availability

Availability of the preferred material is important, especially if you plan to grow shrooms on a large-scale and in the long-term. A material that is not easily available with frustrate your success.

Do basic research in your local market to establish the availability of the various potential materials for your shrooms to find out how easily available each material is. This will help you select the most appropriate material.

3. Fitness for space

While fitness for space may not be such a big factor when you have grinders, it can be a factor in case you don't. When you are operating on a small, non-commercial scale, you need a material that can easily fit within your tiny space – e.g. within a gunny bag, within a drawer or even a small container.

Grains, sawdust, and such other granulated materials can easily fit into small containers. Straws, logs, and such other long fibers will require to be trimmed or ground.

4. Cost

How expensive is your preferred material? It would be necessary for the cost to be economical. You would not like to go for materials that will make the cost of growing your shrooms much higher than the price of buying the same shrooms in the market.

5. The shroom species

Naturally, different species do well on certain specific substrates. Some species do well on dead logs while others do well on straws. Still, others do well on powdery substrates. The best substrate is that which mimics the natural characteristics of a species' preferred substrate.

However, this should not limit you as most shroom species are tolerant of the commonly used substrates such as straws, grains, sawdust, and such like.

Substrate material

There are many substrate materials to choose from. The following are the most widely used substrate materials:

- Agar

- Grains (brown rice grain, brown wheat grain, popcorns, etc.)

- Straws (rye straws, wheat straws, etc.)

- Coir

- Sawdust

- Woodchips/cardboard chips

- Paper pellets

- Hardwood pellets

- Manure

Substrate supplements

Substrate supplements are those compounds that boost the efficacy of the substrate. Common substrate materials include:

- Gypsum (calcium sulfate)

- Lime (calcium carbonate)

- Yeast

- Malt extracts

- Coffee grounds

Treating your substrate

Shrooms are very sensitive to contamination. The contaminants could be physical, chemical, or biological. In most cases, when it comes to the treatment of a substrate, it is to get rid of biological contaminants such as pests, parasites, and disease-causing micro-organisms.

Decontaminating the substrate

Decontamination is the most common treatment of substrates. The following are the two methods that you can use to decontaminate your substrate:

- Pasteurization

- Sterilization

Pasteurizing your substrate

Pasteurization refers to minimizing the amount of micro-organism in the substrate so that they do not outcompete the mycelium in growth.

Different substrate materials will require a slightly different approach to sterilization. However, the common denominator is that you boil the substrate in water or steam it at between 160- and 180-degrees Fahrenheit.

Sterilizing your substrate

Unlike pasteurization that helps to minimize the bad bacteria while sparing good bacteria, sterilization is about killing all micro-organisms – whether good or bad.

The primary difference between the pasteurization approach and the sterilization approach is the temperature. For sterilization, the temperature is put to the extreme provided that the substrate material is not damaged. Typically, sterilization temperate is set above 250 degrees Fahrenheit.

Get the substrate container ready

You can use wooden containers, plastic containers, ceramic containers, and even metallic containers.

The container preparation

Container preparation involves the following steps:

1. Get the right size of container that fits your space layout and the container holder

2. Disinfect the container using a sterilizer such as a hydrogen peroxide, bleach, or 99% isopropyl alcohol. In the case of a metallic container, avoid using bleach or hydrogen peroxide as they can react with the metals to form dangerous acids or compounds.

3. Dry and desiccate the container

4. Encase/insulate the container

Casing

Casing the substrate happens after filling the substrate container but before closing the 'lid'.

Why casing?

The following are the main reasons that make it imperative to case your substrate:

- Protection against rapid evaporation

- Hydrating the substrate

- Conditioning the substrate for pinhead formation

- Providing a conducive environment for beneficial micro-organisms

Casing materials

The material used for casing include:

- Vermiculite

- Perlite

- Peat moss

- Water crystals

Container decontaminants

The following are decontaminants that you can use for containers:

- Isopropyl alcohol

- Hydrogen peroxide

- Paraffin

- Bleach

Materials & tools used for decontamination purposes:

- Surgical hand gloves

- Masks

- Aluminum foil

The container holder

A container holder is any object that holds the container into the right space. This could be a shelf, a hanger, a raised ground platform, or any other holder.

The shelf

A shelf is a great holder for your containers. However, you can still use the shelf as a container by itself. I prefer using the shelf as a holder rather than a container.

Disinfect the wooden shelves using bleach or hydrogen peroxide, or 70% isopropyl alcohol. This will ensure that molds and other micro-organisms on the shelf's surface do not spread into the substrate.

The tray

Trays are great if you love the portability. With a tray, you can easily move the substrate from one site to another. However, make sure that you do not expose your shrooms to contamination while moving the tray from one point to another. Ideally, only move the tray from one spot to another within the secured and decontaminated site.

Trays on the shelf

My best choice is to place the trays on the movable shelf. This allows me to maximize maneuverability.

Hangers on the beam

Hangers are good when your substrate or grow-medium is an elongated plastic bag.

Straight metallic (or wooden) horizontal beams are fixed about 4 feet above the ground (depending on the length of the bags) across the room. These rounded beams can be 2-3 feet apart depending on the diameter of the bags.

These grow bags are placed on a hanger and then the hanger is placed on the beam. The hangers can be spaced about 1.5-2 feet apart depending on the diameter of the bags.

Thus, the shrooms will grow on the cylindrical surface of the bags which already have holes poked for the sprouts.

Raised ground platform

For a very heavy substrate, especially for heavy commercial farming, the ideal container holder is a raised ground platform. The raised platform is necessary where the ground is outdoor but enclosed by a tent or other temporary arrangement.

If indoors, provided that the floor is cemented, you may not need a raised floor. However, just to avoid accidental flooding that could soak the substrate, you can have a raised platform as a matter of precaution. The raised platform is also ideal in case you have rows with substrate placed in gunny bags such that the mushrooms shoot from the top and sideways.

Culture the spores

When it comes to a culture for the spores, you can either acquire ready-made culture, or you can make your own culture.

Acquiring ready-made culture

If you are a beginner, it is preferable to acquire a ready-made culture. If a friend can donate to you, well and good, otherwise, you can easily buy ready-made culture from the shroom shops.

Preparing your own culture

In case you are not going to buy a ready culture (in a grow-kit), you will have to prepare your own culture. This involves fetching the spores and then germinating them on the base substrate.

Fetching the spores

You will need to harvest the spores from the already fruited shrooms. You will need to lay on the ground a medium that will collect the falling spores from the shroom grills. A tissue paper can easily work as the medium for collecting these spores.

Germinating the spores on the base substrate

Once you have collected the spores, you can then prepare them for germination.

Set the planting site

The planting site should be secure, of the right temperate, humidified, and with controlled lighting.

Securing the site

Security is paramount if you want your shrooms to give you optimal yield. You need to secure your shrooms against:

- Unauthorized people – people who are not authorized to access your magic shrine should be kept off. Children are always curious and will be tempted to dig up the substrate, poke holes in it, or even try to pick the sprouts. Both children and adults can infect the site with micro-organisms that may end up harming the mushrooms.

- Pets – pets will not only do the kind of harm that curious children would do, but they could also contain more dangerous micro-organisms than humans.

- Parasites – rodents are the most dangerous big parasites to the shrooms. Apart from rodents such as rats and mice, insects such as ants and worms can cause harm to the shrooms by feeding on them.

To secure the site:

- Enclose it

- Control movements into and out of the enclosure

- Spray the close environs with pesticides

- If the ground is not cemented, raise the platform upon which the substrate and containers are stood on.

Setting the right temperature

Different species require slightly different temperatures to grow and flourish. Furthermore, different stages of growth require different temperatures. However, irrespective of the species, the following are general ranges:

- Incubation period - 28-30°C

- Pinhead formation period - 22-24 °C

- Cropping period - 22-24 °C

Setting the right lighting

Like temperature, lighting requirement varies from species to species and from one stage of growth to another. However, regardless of the species, the following are ideal lighting settings:

- Incubation period – total darkness

- Pinhead formation period – indirect sunlight (or similar illumination from artificial lighting)

- Cropping period - indirect sunlight (or similar illumination from artificial lighting)

Setting the right humidity

Humidity is extremely important. The right humidity will ensure faster growth and optimal production.

The following is the humidity range for the various stages of growth

- Incubation period – 97-100 %

- Pinhead formation period – 97-100 %

- Cropping period - 90 – 95 %

Inoculate your substrate

Inoculating the substrate means to insert the spores into the base substrate (primary substrate).

To inoculate:

1. Create holes into the substrate where you will inject the spores

2. Sterilize the syringe using 99% isopropyl alcohol and dry it

3. Pull the syringe plunger to suck in the spores solution

4. Insert the syringe in one of the holes created and push the plunger to release the spores to release 0.25cc in the hole. Repeat the same for the remaining holes. Make sure that you wipe the syringe using a sterilized cotton swab each time before you make a new injection.

Clean and sterilize the syringe each time you are about to suck in more solutions.

Colonize the territory

To colonize the territory is to allow the mycelium to spread throughout the substrate or at least occupy most of it.

The colonization process takes about 3-4 weeks. This is after 7-14 days taken for the mycelium to start appearing (germinate).

During colonization, all you need is to monitor the conditions to ensure that there is the right temperature, humidity, and lighting. With the right conditions, the mycelium will colonize the entire territory – that is, if the spores were fairly distributed.

The period by which colonization takes place is called the incubation period. During this period, the substrate is placed in a dark place. It rests undisturbed.

Tend to the growth

We have already seen how to set the right condition for the various stages of the shrooms' growth. What is important is to match the right conditions with various growth stages. In this regard, you need to know the expected duration of the various growth periods.

Expected duration for the various growth periods

The duration of each growth period plus the overall growth period depends on the species and the growth conditions. Regardless of the species, growth conditions such as humidity, temperature, and light can greatly alter the duration of each growth stage and the overall growth duration. This is why it is important to ensure optimal growth conditions.

The following is a guideline of the average duration for the various stages of growth:

- Incubation period – 2-4 weeks

- Pinhead formation period – 5-10 days

- Cropping period - 3-7 days

You can see there is a wide range of days for each period. You don't need to worry about whether you are accurate with the incubation period or not. When pinheads start forming, simply know that the incubation period is over.

The cropping period will be ushered in when the pinheads start transforming into caps. Cropping period is the period it takes for the fruit to form and mature. That is, from the beginning of capping to the time of harvesting.

Nurture the fruits

During the cropping period, the fruit will be formed. During this period, the most important condition that you must observe is humidity. The fruit is over 80% moisture. Thus, humidity is needed for the fruit to be fleshy, puffy, and healthy.

Humidity is achieved through spraying water in the air around the fruit. At this stage, you should not water the substrate.

Temperature is also of critical importance. The abnormal temperature will stunt the fruit. The temperature should be right.

PART III: HOW TO HARVEST, TREAT AND STORE YOUR PSILOCYBIN MUSHROOMS

Harvested mushrooms

Photo by Jeremy Bishop / unsplash.com

Overview

Harvesting mushrooms is not a hard task. However, it needs delicate handling to ensure that you do not destroy the mycelium.

Treating and storing the harvested mushroom is also an easy affair. Just like harvesting, it is also not a hard task. What it requires is extra care to make sure that the potency does not inadvertently diminish due to mishandling or poor storage.

In this Part, you are going to learn the simple harvesting techniques plus basic treatment and storage methods that will ensure that you enjoy the magic potency for days, weeks, and even months to come.

Topics covered

- How to harvest your psilocybin mushrooms

- How to cure and store your psilocybin mushrooms

Chapter 7: How to Harvest Your Psilocybin Mushrooms

Mushrooms harvested into a basket

Photo by Carboxaldehyde / pexels.com

The moment has now arrived when your mushroom is ready to reward you for your dedicated, delicate, and tireless effort of tending to them. They are now ready to drive you nuts... and skyrocket you to the cosmos of a new reality.

Yet, you want to continue reaping more from every joule of your energy invested in growing these shrooms plus the money invested in buying the grow-kit. The first yield will give you dividends. But as a shrewd investor, you want to continue earning beyond the dividends. You want to earn a bonus from every other cycle you harvest from the grow-kit after the dividends. To make sure that you earn handsome dividends plus fatty bonuses, I am going to show you how to harvest psilocybin dividends while gaining more from the magical bonuses.

The timing

Not all mushrooms will be ready for picking at the same time. Just as some humans excel in sprinting while others excel in the marathon, some mushrooms will grow faster than others. As a rule of thumb, start harvesting when about three-quarters of your mushrooms are ready.

How do you tell that your mushrooms are ready for harvesting?

For beginners who have not been used to either growing or harvesting mushrooms, it may be quite difficult to tell that their mushrooms are ready for harvesting. Harvesting mushrooms prematurely means that the potency level is not optimized. Harvesting them very late means that there are risks of rotting. You wouldn't like that taste from biting a rotten mushroom.

The following are telling signs that your mushrooms are ready for harvesting:

- **The cap shape:** For most mushroom species, ready mushrooms caps start turning from convex to concave. That is, from turning down to turning up.

- **The veil break**: for those mushrooms that have a veil cover over the gills, watch out for the time the veil begins to break to expose the gills. This signals that the mushrooms are mature and ready for reproduction. By the time the spores start getting released, the more the delay, the lower the potency gets.

- **The spores release**: If you have been late to watch the veil break, or your species require you to just wait slightly after the veil break, watch out for the spores falling. When the spores start to fall, harvest immediately.

- **The darkening edges**: when some mushrooms get mature, the cap edges start darkening. For most mushrooms, the gills start darkening – signaling that spores are mature.

- **The hardening or drying out**: the cap of some species starts hardening or drying out at the edges. The hardening may be accompanied by dryness of the thin cover over the cap or even cracking of this thin cover. However, the hardening or drying out should be the last sign if other signs haven't manifest. This is because, the hardening, and especially drying out manifest over-maturity. Over-maturity means that you are quite late in your harvest.

Why harvest just before the veil breaks?

For maximum potency, harvest your magic mushroom immediately before the veil breaks from the cap or stem. The veil breaks about 5-12 days after the first pins begin to pop-up. The range is quite wide because, apart from variation in species and strains, variations in environmental factors such as temperature, humidity, aeration, and nutrition can affect this period.

If you intend to flush your grow-kit – that is, reuse it for several cycles of growth after the first harvest, then, you must not allow the veil to break.

When the veil breaks and the spores start falling on the substrate, this triggers the mycelium to release a hormone that allows it to stop the fruiting process and start the colonization process. The consequence is that the grow-kit will unlikely produce further flushes when the colonization process begins.

Again, the released spores will taint and darken the still growing mushroom underneath, thus making them aesthetically less appealing to consume or sell.

The picking

Now that you are sure that your mushrooms are mature, the next thing is to pick them. I assume that you are picking them from the grow-kit. However, the procedure is the same, even without a grow-kit.

The tools

- Surgeon's hand gloves – for making sure that the substrate is not contaminated during harvesting. Make sure that your hands are cleaned, dried, and sanitized before putting on gloves

- Tweezers – for small shrooms that your fingers can hardly reach

- Small brush – for wiping the substrate off the base of the shroom once pulled out

- Container – for putting in harvested mushrooms

Materials

- Gloves – to cover the hands

- Sterilizer – to sterilize the hands and the harvest container

The picking method

Use Twist-and-Pull technique

Procedure

1. Plunge your index finger or thumb to the base of the stem

2. Gently twist and pull the stem until it starts loosening from the substrate. Gradually apply more pull force in case the stem is not pulling up after loosening. Take care not to apply excessive force as this may end up harming the mycelium, thus making it difficult to optimize yield from further flushes. Use small tweezers to pick up smaller mushrooms that may be hard to handle with your hands

3. Use a small brush to gently wipe off loose substrate matter that may cling to the base of the pulled-up mushroom.

4. Repeat the process for other mushrooms till you can harvest all mushrooms.

Once you are done with harvesting your shrooms, the next thing is to store them in such a way that optimizes the potency while rewarding you with extra benefits.

Chapter 8: How to Cure and Store Your Psilocybin Mushrooms

picked mushrooms

Photo by Albarubescens / CC BY-SA 4.0

You can consume your magic mushrooms while still fresh. You can extend the shelf-life of this freshness by three days. You can achieve this through refrigeration. However, every extra day of refrigeration erodes the shroom's potency – not forgetting the increased risk of molding, rotting, and contamination.

Thus, if you want to retain potency while stretching your consumable shrooms' shelf-life, the best option is to dry the shrooms. Dried shrooms have the added advantage of higher potency per gram (gross). You will have almost 10 times more potency per gram from dry shrooms compared to a gram of fresh shrooms. This also increases the ease of packaging and portability of your shrooms.

How to dry magic mushrooms

There are three main ways to dry your shrooms:

- Air-drying

- Sun-drying

- Oven-drying

Air-drying

In air drying, you simply expose your shrooms to a fresh supply of dry air at room temperature. This will take the longest period to dry. However, you can accelerate the drying by slightly increasing the temperature of the circulating air.

Sun-drying

This is the most practiced method of drying during summer, especially in the tropical climate where there is plenty of intense sunshine.

Sun-drying relies on the sun rays to dry the mushroom.

The biggest advantage of sun-drying is that your shrooms get more injection of Vitamin D. Thus, their nutritional value increases.

Oven-drying

In case air-drying and sun-drying are not feasible, especially during winter in the cold climates, then oven-drying becomes the most preferred choice.

To oven-dry:

1) Place the shrooms on a paper towel and set each shroom apart from the other

2) Dry the shrooms for about 5 days or until dry while still spread on the paper towel

How to store magic mushrooms

Once your shrooms are cured (or dried), it is time to store them.

Storing fresh mushrooms

Fresh mushrooms can be stored for up to 3 days in a refrigerator. Storing fresh mushrooms for more than three days will significantly reduce their potency. Also, the risk of spoilage goes high.

Storing dry mushrooms

The plastic food container is the cheapest and easiest way to store your dry mushrooms.

Procedure:

1. To ensure that the mushroom does not retain or acquire moisture from the sealed-in air, lay a clean paper towel on the inside bottom and inner sides of the container.

2. Put in your dry mushrooms.

3. Optionally, place another clean paper towel on top of the dry mushrooms.

4. Keep the container in a cool dry place. Preferably, keep the container on a shelf or aerated cupboard.

PART IV: HOW TO CONSUME YOUR DELICIOUS PSILOCYBIN MUSHROOMS

psychedelic tea time

Overview

The climax of your effort comes in reaping its rewards. You have grown and nurtured your shrooms. You've given them the tender care that they deserve.

It is now time that they give you that tender psychedelic love that you desire. This is the best way they can thank you and appreciate you for your effort. However, they only speak through magic. Thus, as their experienced spokesperson, I take this opportunity to unveil their gratitude – a momentous trip to paradise.

Topics covered

- Your shroom consumption methods

- How to take a dose of your magic

- How to savor your meal-time with shroom edibles recipes

Chapter 9: Your Shroom Consumption Methods

When it comes to consuming your magic shrooms, be creative enough to boost your enjoyment and thus keep monotony at bay.

Several consumption methods exist that you can employ in the consumption of your shrooms.

Factors determining your choice of consumption

Several factors determine your choice of consumption. The following are several factors;

- **Purpose of consumption** – consuming shrooms for recreational purposes might mean a different way of consuming it as opposed to consuming shrooms for therapeutic purposes. For example, for recreational purposes, eat edibles. However, for medicinal purposes, swallow capsules.

- **Convenience** – convenience in terms of portability will give preference to one way of consumption as opposed to another. Capsules are the most portable form of cannabis consumption compared to other forms.

- **Durability and effectiveness of potency** – some methods of consuming shrooms are more potent than others. For example, taking shroom capsules is more potent than raw ingestion (eating raw).

- **Reactionary time** – if you desire a fast reaction from shrooms, it is preferable to take in capsules. However, if you desire a slower reaction, then, edibles become the preferred option.

How to consume shrooms

The following are the common methods of consuming shrooms:

- Raw (direct) ingestion

- Shroom edibles

- Shroom powders

- Shroom capsules

- Shroom extracts

Raw (direct) ingestion

Eating raw shrooms is a common practice. Those who eat raw do it mostly because it is time-saving. However, eating raw increases your chances of nausea. This is because, despite the magic effect, psilocybes are not tasty. Most psilocybes have a rather bitter and unpleasant taste.

Shroom edibles

Psilocybin mushrooms are just as edible as other mushrooms, only that they have medicinal properties and a rather bitter taste.

Shroom edibles are common these days. Common edibles include:

- Brews and beverages – tea, coffee, chocolate, etc.

- Crunchy snacks – chocolates, cookies, crackers, popcorns, nut mixes, gummy bears, chews, etc.

- Sweets – lollipops, other sweets, etc.

Read Chapter 11 for a collection of delicious shroom edibles recipes.

Shroom powders

Shroom powders are easy to make. You simply need to dry your shrooms and then pound them into powder. To pound, put the shrooms into a zip-lockable plastic bag and then start pounding using a pestle. Once they attain the powder form, you can place them into a powder dispenser.

Whenever you want to use the shroom powder, simply sprinkle it on your preferred edible. You can also use the powder to make teas just as you use powdered herbs such as ginger and vanilla.

Shroom capsules

Shroom capsules are filled with dried shrooms. You can either buy them or make them yourself. All you need to make your shroom capsules is to buy the empty capsule casings from the pharmacy and use a spatula to fill in the measured quantity.

Make sure that the measurement is fairly accurate for the same type of capsules so that you can have a fairly uniform effect.

Shroom extracts

Psilocybin (or even psilocin) can be extracted from shrooms. This is by far the most concentrated form of shroom magic.

These extracts get consumed as sublingual. However, shroom extracts are not so common as edibles and capsules. This is mainly because of the rather long process involved in deriving the extracts.

Shroom extracts are often used as sublingual. Sublingual refers to entry into the bloodstream via the mouth blood vessels, more so, under the tongue. Psilocin can easily be absorbed by mouth's blood vessels. Common forms of shroom consumption through sublingual include:

- The Magic Tinctures

- The Crystals of God

The Magic Tinctures (Holy Waters)

Tinctures are a liquid form of psilocybin extracts obtained through alcohol-based extraction. As such, they contain a small volume of alcohol in them.

How to make magic tinctures

Tools required:

- Small desk fan

- Dust pollen masks

- Bottles with tight caps

- Filter funnel

- Drinking glass

- 10cc syringe

Material used:

- Dried shrooms

- 200 proof ethyl alcohol

Procedure:

1) Cool-dry the mushrooms using a desiccant. Let them be ready for pulverization.

2) Pour the dried mushrooms in a zip-locked plastic bag and pound them with a pestle to pulverize

3) Pour the pulverized mushrooms into a bottle. Tighten the leak-proof bottle-top to seal

4) Pour in the bottle the 200 proof ethyl alcohol till the mixture becomes slurry

5) Stir the content by shaking the bottle. Let the content settle for 24 hours. Afterward, shake it often so that the psilocybin can get off the dry matter and dissolve into the alcohol

6) After another 24 hours frequent shaking, use the filter funnel to isolate the alcohol

7) Pour the remaining slurry into the cloth filter and squeeze it to extract more alcohol into the drinking glass

8) Keep the extracted alcohol into another bottle

9) Soak the extracted shroom material from the filter in more alcohol and repeat steps (5) to (8) for more rounds of filtration

10) Put together all the extracted alcohol into a glass

11) Instigate faster evaporation by using the fan to blow over the glass. You can even use a clean hairdryer to provide hot air that can quicken the evaporation rate.

12) Continue evaporating the alcohol until you attain the required concentration. As a rule of thumb, 1g of dried mushroom should produce 1cc of tincture or less. If 3g can produce 1cc, then that will be a much higher concentration. However, this depends on the potency of the dried shrooms.

13) Store the tincture into a screw-cap bottle and keep it
    in the freezer.

14) Use the syringe to dispense the tincture. The syringe
    is ideal because of the more accurate calibration.

The Crystals of God

Crystals of God refers to the powdery crystals of psilocin obtained through the evaporation and crystallization process. Due to their solid form, the Crystals of God lasts longer than the 'Holy Waters'.

The Crystals of God are, in essence, dried Tears of God. Thus, to create these crystals, you build upon the tincture process above.

The crystallization procedure:

1. Pour some few drops of hydrochloric acid into the tincture to achieve a pH level of 3.0

2. Evaporate the acidic content to one-tenth its volume

3. Add paint thinner, cigarette lighter or other nonpolar solvent and gently mix

4. Set the solution for some few hours

5. Free the solution and then pour out the liquid solvent. Alternatively, use the syringe to suck off the floating layer of the solvent after the solution has settled and the layers formed.

6. Gradually add acetone to what is left to remove the remaining solvent. To achieve this, an extra layer will form once the solution with acetone settles. The lower layer will be darker, while the upper layer will be yellowish-greenish.

7. Suck off the top layer using the syringe.

8. Add more acetone. Gently mix, let it settle for some minutes, and remove the acetone layer by sucking it off using the syringe. A dark, sticky residue will be left.

9. Collect the dark sticky residue into a flatter based wide container just to form a thin layer and let it dry. The thin layer is required to facilitate rapid evaporation. Crystals will start forming.

10. Weigh the crystals to determine their potency.

Note: The thickness of the dark layer will determine the evaporation rate and the size of the crystals. The slower the evaporation rate, the bigger the crystals will be.

Now, the crystals of God are ready for consumption.

Chapter 10: How to Take a Dose of Your Magic

Psilocybin is a powerful drug. Thus, like other drugs, you not only need to ensure that you take the right dosage but also take it responsibly.

While the same dosage may have a different impact on different people, there is a universal dosage scale that anyone can safely use before gaining experience of what works for him/her.

The dosing scale

It is hard to have a precise dosing scale since the magic potency varies from species to species. Furthermore, the effect of this potency varies from individual to individual, depending on one's body metabolism and experience.

Dry scale

Nonetheless, the following is a dosage scale for dried stems and powder. The scale is derived based on the intended outcome:

- Party dose: 2–3g

- Creative dose: 0.5–1g

- Micro-dose: 0.15–0.3g

Fresh scale

As a rule of thumb, a dry scale is just a tenth of a fresh scale. Thus, for every dry dose, multiply by 10 to get an equivalent fresh dose.

Thus, for fresh consumption:

- Party dose: 20–30g

- Creative dose: 5–10g

- Micro-dose: 1.5–3g

Apart from this scale that is based on the purpose and the intent of consumption, we can also classify the dosage based on whether it is light, medium, or heavy (strong).

Light Dose

Generally, a light dose is about 0.25g to 0.4g. However, this is not a rigid measurement. The most important measure is the effect it generates.

In terms of effect, a light dose is a minimum threshold that brings the user the magic benefits such as mental clarity, mental acuity, and focus but without causing a hallucinogenic effect.

To some users, there will be a light sensation of chill accompanied by the slight vividness of colors. Some users may experience a starry vision while others may experience a unique 'mushroom aura'.

Medium Dose

A medium dose range is between 1.0g and 2.5g. However, like all mushroom doses, the effect varies. Thus, this is just but a rule of thumb. With experience, you will be able to establish your medium-dose based on your experience.

The effects will be a better guide. For a medium dose, you will experience physical symptoms such as dilation of the pupils, dream-like images, and open-eyed visuals.

For most psilonauts, a medium dose opens up the mind to philosophical thoughts and a sense of enlightenment. This can be accompanied by wavy mood swings between euphoria (peak) and dysphoria (trough). The emotional connection also gets augmented.

Heavy Dose

A heavy dose is for experienced heavy-lifters. In this scenario, you are not riding a motorbike as in the light dose, nor a sports car as in the medium dose, but a heavy truck.

In the heavy dose, you carry the full force of the mushroom. It is a full dose. Here, the creative momentum is in full gear.

A heavy dose ranges between 2.0g and 3.5g. Like an experienced truck driver, you must have endurance muscle to navigate the tough terrain that is your trip. The field is wide open, and it is upon you to craft your path.

In the heavy dose, every experience is put to the limit – both positive and negative. If you have a chance for a positive experience, it will be a great positive experience. But, in the unfortunate event that you have a negative experience, it can be a hellish experience.

To mitigate the potential risks of a bad trip, it is important to take adequate preparation. Cultivate your mind for positivity through mindfulness meditation, Neuro-Linguistic Programming, Positive Affirmation, and even Creative visualization. Your state of mind before taking the heavy dose, has a great influence on the kind of trip you will encounter – be it dreams or nightmares.

Physically, if you are not experienced enough, you will need to prepare for negative reactions such as strong nausea. You will probably need some eyeshades just to cover up your inflated pupil from prying eyes. You must also prepare yourself for shocks of the rapid and jarring effects at the start of your trip before the trip smoothens out.

Thus, if you are a beginner, stay away from the heavy lifting. Start light and get accustomed to it before switching to the medium gear.

Furthermore, when you venture into heavy lifting, whether experienced or not, it is important to have a trip-sitter with you. You also need to be in a more familiar environment or an environment adequately prepared for the psychedelic trip, such as psychedelic retreat sites. Also, don't forget to carry your First-Aid kit – just in case you encounter a bad trip that turns awry.

Whichever the dose – whether be it light, medium, or heavy, take it responsibly to mitigate the risk of negative experiences.

How to responsibly fuel your trip to paradise

We have already seen that the same level of a dose can have a different effect on different people. Thus, for a beginner, you can never assume that a given dose will not have serious psychoactive effects. So, it is important to always prepare yourself for the trip. Even the most experienced trip-goer does preparation – only more efficiently.

Pre-trip responsibility

Like an astronaut preparing for the space mission, you have to exhibit the very same thoroughness as a psilonaut. You are responsible for your mission. Thus, you must take pre-trip responsibility seriously as it is the one that will determine whether you will successfully reach your intended destination or not.

You have to take the following pre-trip actions:

1. *Cast your trip in the mind*

We have also seen that the greatest preparation starts in the mind – like every other journey. Thus, you must set your mind right. A right mindset will more likely map out a more scenic trip. The map work is done in your mind. In this regard, we've seen the importance of mindfulness, meditation, and creative visualization. Practice them in advance, more so when this is your first trip outside the normal reality.

2. *Make sure that you are qualified for the trip*

The first and foremost thing is to note that the psychedelic trip is for ADULTS ONLY. Thus, if you are below 21 years of age, please, don't board the psychedelic vessel. The legal age of adulthood is 18 years for most jurisdictions. But the legal age is not the same as biological age as some people mature earlier or later than others. 21 years is a sure age in terms of biological maturity.

Apart from being biologically mature, you need to be an ADULT OF SOUND MIND. If you are a mentally unstable person, don't board the psychedelic spacecraft. Furthermore, if you are a trip-sitter, don't do sitting for someone who is not of sound mind, you will bear full blame for the consequences.

While being mentally fit is paramount, there is an exception for certain mental disorders that have been proven to be healed by psilocybin. However, in this case, you need the help of a qualified medical practitioner.

Physical fitness is also important. You are a psilonaut. Thus, don't board the spacecraft to paradise if you have serious infection or disease. Heal first, unless it is a disease that has been proven to be remedied by psilocybin.

3. *Have a trip-sitter ready to co-pilot you*

Don't go on the trip alone. Have someone sober to co-pilot just in case you lose control of the spacecraft. You need someone to help you read the map, navigate the path, and ensure that you are safely destined.

The person you choose to be your trip-sitter should be someone you trust and is interested in your welfare. Furthermore, the person should be an experienced tripper.

4. *Have the right food and drinks on your trip*

You never know how long your trip could take. You never know how pangs of hunger would behave. As we suggested, the best way to have an impactful trip is to start it on an empty stomach. We also suggested that the trip can take up to 8 hours while in space. You are not on a fasting mission unless you have deliberately decided on that purpose. Thus, while on the trip, you will need to quench your thirst, hydrate your body, and nourish your gut. However, it is a bit challenging when it comes to food. Most psilonaut would rather not eat while on the trip. This is because eating can trigger or aggravate nauseatic sensations. The increased sensitivity of the gut as a result of psilocybin makes your gut more likely to reject certain types of foods.

Apart from having plenty of clean drinking water, you also need to have energizing food. This is to keep you strong and stable as the spacecraft's motion can take you off-balance.

You can also have some sugar-containing drinks for quick effect just in case you experience acute fatigue. However, sugar-containing drinks can shorten your trip. Anyway, a shorter trip is good if you are a beginner.

5. *Keep your environment safe, secure, and serene*

Avoid a cluttered environment. Keep off from hazards such as running machines, flammable substances, a toxic substance, slippery surface, insecure heights, and such others.

To experience serenity, switch off your communication gadgets. This is not the time to risk receiving the bad news that will make you agitated or even good news that will make you overly excited. Also, make sure that in the next 24 hours from the moment you begin the trip is free from important or official appointments.

Avoid taking a trip to crowded places or places with lots of strangers. Strangers may be offended by your weird conduct and become aggressive. Others may seek to take advantage of your condition in case you are out of control, and you have no reliable trip-sitter. As such, avoid tripping while partying in festivals or carnivals.

6. *Keep off other drugs*

Those who are used to taking LSD and mixing this intake with other drugs such as cannabis, tobacco, and alcohol would be more inclined to extend the same to their psilocybin trip. However, the experience may not be the same. It could make matters worse. Your spacecraft could easily go off-path and land you in hell instead of your deserved paradise.

Avoid combining psilocybin with other drugs. Psilocybin likes monopolizing your experience and is extremely jealous of unnecessary competition.

Pro-trip responsibility

While on the trip, even though your shuttle is on auto-mode, there are things that you can still be able to do.

The following are actions that you have to take as part of your pro-trip responsibility:

1. Drink plenty of water

As a consequence of your body's reaction to psilocybin, you are more likely to dehydrate if you don't drink plenty of water. Already, you took the shroom on an empty stomach, thus, dehydration is the one thing you cannot afford on your trip.

Before your body becomes tolerant of psilocybin, it treats it as a toxin. This is why it uses plenty of water to flush off this 'toxin' from your body.

One fallacy that some have is the belief that drinking plenty of water will dilute the psychedelic experience. This is not the case. Even by drinking plenty of water, you will still experience the same kind of potency. Furthermore, your brain requires to be hydrated to function well. Dehydration can be counterproductive to your intended brain prowess.

2. Keep off the temptation to become tipsy while on the trip

Those who are accustomed to drinking alcohol, especially after consuming marijuana, would more likely be tempted to take alcohol while on the psychedelic trip.

The magical effect of the psilocybin mushroom is to accelerate switch over from one thought to another. This high-speed acceleration is what makes the trip enjoyable. However, when you take alcohol while on the trip, it decelerates rather than accelerating your thought-transformation speed. You may start experiencing a sluggish looping of the same thought. This brings a bad experience.

Alcohol is a depressant. It depresses your thoughts and moods. It is the antithesis of psilocybin. So, no need to take it.

3. *Take comfort in the journey*

Once psilocin seizes you and once the shuttle has triggered, you are on auto-mode. Take comfort in your experience by relaxing your nerves and just exploring the scenic visions as they unveil within. Just enjoy the heaven as it clears the fog and opens up the clouds.

Some scenes may be scary along the journey. Don't freak out. Don't let fear bring hell. And some scenes may be profoundly magnificent, don't try to cling to them just enjoy and pass - for more awaits you.

Free your nerves in order to experience the total joy that comes with mental freedom. There is simply no greater freedom than the freedom of your mind. Seize the moment and enjoy it to the fullest.

4. *Take care of your social needs*

Social needs during the trip depend so much on your personality type. For example, most introverts would desire more privacy during the trip and thus would tend to stay alone. On the other hand, most extroverts would desire much closer companionship. However, in certain instances, some introverts become more extroverted, while some extroverts become more introverted.

If you are on your first trip, you may not be able to determine your social needs in advance. But, after several trips, you will be able to tell whether you desire companionship during your trip or not. However, as a beginner, it is prudent that you have a trip-sitter. You can also one or two people you trust to come along with you on your trip. If during the first trip you realize that you need no company, not bad – at least you wouldn't have risked encountering the vagaries of undesired loneliness.

While on the trip, it is important that you communicate and also express your social needs. Some people may want to chat with you when you don't feel like – please tell them in a non-offensive way. Others may want more intimacy while you don't even want to be touched – please let them know. You are on this trip to enjoy it, not to tolerate avoidable displeasures.

5. *Flow with the waves*

There will be high tides and low tides. There will be peaks and troughs. Don't try to flatten the picks and fill the troughs. Simply move with the waves. Keep the motion. Go with the momentum. A safe harbor awaits you... in the end.

While it will be a bit hard for you to flatten the peak, there will be a temptation to gobble up more psilocybin to fill the trough. Be warned. Don't attempt to fill the trough. You never know the magic power of the hidden undercurrents. Tides can easily rise so quickly to overwhelm your vessel. Be satisfied with the motion... and you will become an experienced psilosailor the more you stay calm during your psilovoyage.

Dealing with a bad trip

Experienced astronauts know that not all space missions achieve success. Some turn awry. The same happens with psychedelic trips. While most trips get trippers to paradise, some trips can land trippers in hell.

 In the unfortunate case of a bad trip, the trip-sitter must take charge to help navigate the trip shuttle to a safe landing.

The following are important things that a trip-sitter must do:

- Keep the focus on the tripper.

- Take the tripper to a quiet and calming environment where the tripper can sit down for calm breathing. Heart racing is common on most bad trips. Slowing down the breath-rate helps to bring back the heartbeat to normalcy.

- Help the tripper see that the bad trip is not a never-ending endeavor. In most cases, the tripper has lost the essence of time, and one minute could seem a whole day. Fear and desperation heighten when the tripper feels that the situation is not ending. This can cause anguish and even physical agitation.

- Encourage the tripper to drink sweet beverages. Sugar helps to bring down the psychedelic effect

- In case the tripper is extremely agitated and cannot calm down, or you feel that you are becoming overwhelmed, or that the tripper is in danger, please call emergency services for help. This will enable the tripper to get professional medical attention. Explain to emergency attendants the state of the tripper and what triggered that particular state so that they can provide an appropriate remedy.

Post-trip

Now that you are back to the world, subtly supercharged, you can be a witness to what it means to come back from beyond-this-world. Sometimes you can feel like an alien to your old reality. You are transformed, even in the most infinitesimal way. While physically you may appear the same, your mind is no longer the same. You are in a new normal.

What do you do?

It is time to reflect on the trip experience. I hope it was a trip to paradise. I hold it so. It is time to enliven your paradise here on earth. Keep expanding your alien territory through more trip experiences. And if you are a one who loves the company while on the trip, keep recruiting new psilonauts. And if you are a good storyteller, keep people inspired by your trip stories.

You are now more earthed than before. When the self DIED, it meant that you are newly connected with the nature of beings and the nature of things. Be mindful. Spread compassion. Nurture the good that is beyond the self. Your trip was about exploring heaven beyond the self. Spread this heaven here on earth – in joy, in peace, and harmony.

How to engage your trip gear

While cruising on your trip to paradise, you can engage various gears along the way – depending on your dose, experience, and circumstances.

If you are a beginner, the dose you take may push you to a certain gear – even unintended one. However, when you are an experienced tripper, you can manipulate the dose to achieve the desired gear.

The following are the 5 major gears that you can engage to boost your speed range:

Gear 1

This is the *focus gear*.

The first gear ushers at a pretty slow speed. This is the best gear for learners. It is also the right gear for those on micro-dosing to increase mental acuity, think convergently, heighten focus and concentration, and boost productivity.

Taking a trip on this gear will expose you to a luminous experience where you start seeing the surrounding ambiance and colors brightening up. The music starts becoming more intense. You also feel a bit high with a more vibrant spirit. You are now able to see your environment in detail and with greater clarity.

Gear 2

This is the ***creativity gear***.

On this gear, you move at a slightly higher speed than the first gear. Your mind starts being bombarded with great ideas. You are thinking fast and in more detail. The colors become brighter, and the ambiance warmer. You feel the music not just intense but throbbing inside your body. Closed-eye visuals begin to cast, plus more animated images start popping up. You become psilosophical.

Gear 3

This is the ***ego dissolution gear***.

It is where you find that your Self DIED.

Tripping on this gear dissolves your ego. You are no longer yourself. There is neither yesterday nor tomorrow. Yesterday died, and tomorrow ceased to be born. Today only comes in momentary drips. You are seized by the moment of now. Time has become an illusion. There is no difference between one minute and one hour. They are both illusions.

The visual impact has become intense. Your pupil is both inflated and dilated. You are now beyond the normal reality. Every form looks distorted and unreal. There is mild hallucination. You are in a new world... experiencing a new reality. You are now a psiloangel.

Gear 4

This is the **object deformation gear**.

Tripping on this gear dissolves the form of objects around you. Objects begin to lose their form within your sight. You can even witness a dog deforming into a dry leaf. You can even witness fence posts deforming into an ostrich that starts talking to you.

On this gear, you experience strong hallucinations. There is an absolute loss of realism. There is a complete percepticide. The magicians in the shrooms have taken over your world. You are being bombarded with one miracle after the other. You are now a psiloghost.

Gear 5

This is the ***universal oneness gear***.

You are in perfect union with everything and every being. Boundaries dissolve. The world that you have always known ceased to exist and DIED with the self. Normal sense, common sense, and logic have already departed from you. You have melted into the universe, and there are only one universal being and one universal intelligence. The power of logic control that you previously exercised simply dissipated into the universe. You are now the omnipotent, omniscient, and omnipresent. You are a psilogod.

Chapter 11: How to Savor Your Meal-time With Shroom Edibles Recipes

As we have seen in Chapter 9, one of the ways to consume your shrooms is through edibles. Common edibles include:

- Brews and beverages – tea, coffee, chocolate, etc.

- Crunchy snacks – chocolates, cookies, crackers, popcorns, nut mixes, gummy bears, chews, etc.

- Sweets – lollipops, other sweets, etc.

Shroom brews and beverages

Brews and beverages are a great way to launch your trip while ensuring that you are sufficiently hydrated. Furthermore, if you are micro-dosing for purposes of work productivity, taking shroom beverages early in the morning as your breakfast can make you have a great mental experience as you work.

Tea is by far the most popular shroom beverage. However, there are many other shroom beverages such as shroom chocolates, shroom juices, shroom smoothies, among others.

How to prepare your psychedelic tea

psychedelic mush tea

For tea lovers, psychedelic tea made from shrooms is the best way to jumpstart your day. It is also the best way to neutralize the awful taste of the shrooms on your tongue. Yes, chewing raw shrooms is not an experience that many can cope with. So, tea becomes the savior in this regard.

Dried shroom tea

In the dried shroom tea, you used dried shrooms, either chopped or powdered (or both).

Utensils

Whichever kind of tea you will need to make, the following are basic utensils that you will need

- Teapot

- Kettle

- Mug

- Strainer

- spoons

Ingredients

Basic ingredients:

- dried and chopped shrooms (Shroom powder is preferred)

- Tea leaves (tea bags preferred)

- Boiled water

Optional ingredients:

- sugar

- Honey

- Orange juice (lemon or citrus can also do)

Preparation

1. Pour water into the kettle and heat to the boiling point

2. Put your preferred dose of shrooms powder (or dried and chopped shrooms) into the teapot

3. Pour the boiling water into the shroomed teapot and let settle for a quarter an hour while stirring occasionally and gently

4. Strain into cups, add optional ingredients to your taste and serve

Note: The dosage varies per your needs. For a light dose, you can have 1 gram of shroom powder per cup. For a heavy dose, you can have 5 grams of shroom powder per cup. If you are a beginner, start with the light dose, especially if you are going to add citric fruit juice (citrus, lemon, or orange)

Fresh shroom tea

For preparing fresh shroom tea, utensils and procedures are the same. The only difference is that you are using fresh chopped shrooms as opposed to dry shrooms.

When it comes to fresh shrooms, use about 10 times more quantity of shrooms as you would do for dry shrooms. If you were to use 1g of dry shrooms, use 10gms of fresh shrooms.

Reaping the bonus from your tea

Yes, the first round of tea gives you the dividends for your psychedelic investment. However, it doesn't stop there. If you used chopped mushrooms, then, there is a lot more psilocybin trapped in there after straining. There will still be some traps in the powder, but much less.

So, with chopped shrooms, take advantage of the bonus.

Just put all the shroom residues from the first round into the teapot and repeat steps (1), (2), and (4) above.

The bonus round may not be as potent as the dividend round. Thus, to keep the same level of potency, you may opt to add about one-quarter of the initial dose to the residue to up the potency. Make sure that this addition is a fine powder so that it able to release almost all its potency into the teapot.

Note: If you desire a second round, it is preferable to use chopped shrooms rather than powdered shrooms in the first round. The advantage is that there will be more potency in the residue of the chopped shrooms. This potency will be released quicker into the teapot during the second round than in the first round. Thus, if you desire a second round in quicker succession, this is the way to go.

Truffle Tea

In preparing the Truffle tea, you will need the same utensils as in preparing shroom tea. You will also employ the same procedures.

The only difference is that you will replace shrooms with chopped truffles.

Ginger Twist Tea

Ginger Twist Tea includes ginger and orange juice as basic ingredients. Like tea leaves, ginger is a stomach relaxant and thus helps to remedy stomach upsets. It can also help to relieve nausea. Orange is a great remedy for nausea. Taking orange will help you feel less nausea.

You can either prepare ginger twist tea with dried shrooms or fresh shrooms. The utensils used, and the procedure is the same. The only addition is ginger to the ingredients. Add ginger mixed with shrooms or truffles. Freshly grated ginger matches well with fresh chopped shrooms/truffles. Powdered ginger matches well with powdered shrooms.

In case you are prone to or more susceptible to nausea, use dry powdered ginger instead of fresh ginger.

How to prepare your psychedelic chocolate drink

Chocolate is a rich drink. It not only has great nutritional value but also anti-oxidants that helps to keep premature aging at bay. Thus, combining chocolate with shrooms not only keeps you healthier and happier but also younger.

Utensils

- Teapot

- Kettle

- Mug

- Strainer

- spoons

Ingredients

Basic ingredients:

- shroom powder

- chocolate powder

- Boiled water

- Sugar/honey (optional)

Preparation

1. Pour water into the kettle and heat to the boiling point

2. Put your preferred dose of shrooms powder into the teapot

3. Pour the boiling water into the shroomed teapot and let settle for a quarter an hour while stirring occasionally and gently

4. Strain into cups

5. Add chocolate and sugar to your taste

6. Serve and drink

How to prepare your psychedelic yogurt

If you love yogurt and shrooms, a blend of the two can be a scintillating experience.

Preparation:

1. Put fruit yogurt into a small jug

2. Sprinkle in a measured dose of powdered shrooms

3. Stir aggressively using a whisk

4. Set for about 15 minutes in a refrigerator

5. Serve

Cherry yogurt works best as cherries are great at suppressing the shrooms' awful taste.

How to prepare your psychedelic juice

Fruit juice is extremely refreshing, especially chilled juice during a hot summer season. Adding a dose of psilocybin to the fruit juice can make your drinking sensations more accentuated.

Preparation:

1. Pour your preferred fruit juice into a small jug

2. Sprinkle in a measured dose of powdered shrooms

3. Stir gently and let settle for about 15 minutes while stirring occasionally

4. Use a strainer to sieve the juice into another jug

5. Refrigerate the sieved for about 30 minutes to chill

6. Pour into glasses and serve

How to prepare your favorite lemon elixir

Lemon juice elixir is not only delicious but also relaxing. It works well in toning your gut, thus making you feel a lot more comfortable.

When blending with truffles or shrooms, the cruising speed of your spacecraft not only gets quickly accelerated, but your gut is spared the nauseating resistance to the trip.

Preparation:

1. Chop the shrooms or truffles into small pieces

2. Pour the chops into a mug and squeeze in the lemon juice

3. Set the mug content for 15 minutes, occasionally stirring it.

4. Pour in some sterilized or boiled but cooled drinking water and set for a further 15 minutes, occasionally stirring it

5. Enjoy your elixir

The benefit of shroom tea over chewing the dry shrooms

The following are the key benefits of shroom tea over chewing the dry shrooms:

1. While chewing dry shrooms will start you at normal acceleration, shroom tea starts you at much higher

acceleration. Thus, you achieve optimal speed much faster with shroom tea than the chewable.

2. If you intend to switch gears from gear 1 to say gear 2 and then 3 in quick succession, then shroom tea will smoothly switch you over.

3. Shroom tea neutralizes the awful taste of psilocybin in the shrooms. This decreases the degree of nausea.

4. Tea leaves are naturally gut relaxants. Thus, when you add tea leaves to your shrooms, you mitigate the potential effects of stomach upsets. Unless your gut is hypersensitive to psilocybin, you will be able to avoid stomach upsets altogether.

5. There will be quicker absorption of shroom tea as opposed to chewed substance that will need laborious digestion. This absorption can be greatly accelerated by adding citric fruit juice to your tea. The longer the digestion takes place, the higher is the risk of stomach upsets and nausea.

The benefit of citric fruit juice in your shroom beverages

Adding citrus fruit juice such as lemon or orange facilitates the conversion of psilocybin into psilocin right in the teacup rather than waiting for this to happen in the gut. Thus, the trip receives a big acceleration boost right from the sip. However, the trip lasts shorter than the normal case. You also need to be cautious since the sudden acceleration may push you off-guard. Be prepared for this.

Shroom smoothies

Smoothies have a great way of smoothening your alimentary canal and soothing your gut. If you love drinking smoothies, then, you can still enjoy shroom smoothies as part of your psychedelic trip.

Apple-Berry shroom smoothie and Banana-chocolate smoothie are some of the most loved smoothies by psilonaut. This is because of the effect their ingredients have on the gut, especially when it comes to mitigating the effects of nausea.

Apple-Berry Shroom Smoothie

Ingredients:

- ½ glass strawberries (frozen)

- 1 glass raspberry sherbert

- 1 glass apple juice

- 1 ½ glasses lemonade

- Double dose powder of magic shrooms

Preparation

1. Pour all your fluid ingredients into a blender

2. Add the frozen strawberries

3. Pulse-blend the ingredients for 45 seconds

4. Switch the blender's power button to medium range and blend further until the mixture becomes flawlessly smooth

5. Sprinkle in the magic powder and blend further for about 30 seconds just to mix

Banana-Chocolate smoothie

Ingredients:

- 1 glass almond milk (unsweetened)

- 2 pitted dates

- 1 frozen ripe banana

- 1 fresh ripe banana

- 1 teaspoon of protein powder (your favorite)

- 1 ½ tablespoon cacao powder

- 1 dose of magic shroom powder

Preparation:

1. pour all the ingredients into the blender

2. blend until flawlessly smooth

3. pour the smoothie into a glass and serve

Crunchy shroom snacks

Love crunchy snacks? Well, you can also crunch your shrooms as part of your snacks. Shrooms are naturally soft, even when dried. So, to make them crunchy, include them as ingredients in your favorite crunchy snack.

Chocolate is a great ingredient for crunchies, especially chocolate bars. As we have said earlier, it becomes even more important when it comes to conditioning the gut to be more receptive to psilocybin.

I have provided for you Chocolate trip recipe, chocolate truffle recipe, and energy balls recipe to open up your creative mind to more creative recipes.

Chocolate trip recipe

Equipment:

- Microwave oven

- Cooking mold (dinosaur mold is ideal)

- Bowl (for melting the chocolate and mixing it with the shroom powder)

Ingredients:

- Milk chocolate bar

- A dose of magic shroom powder

Preparation:

1. Melt a sizeable portion of the chocolate bar in the oven

2. Gradually sprinkle the magic powder into the melted chocolate while gently stirring

3. Once uniformly stirred, allow it to settle and cool. Make sure that the chocolate doesn't solidify

4. Pour the viscous chocolate onto the mold

5. Place the mold in the fridge for it to solidify

6. Savor your psychedelic chocolate at your convenience

Chocolate truffles

Equipment:

- Microwave oven

- Cooking mold (dinosaur mold is ideal)

- Bowl (for melting the chocolate and mixing it with the shroom powder)

Ingredients:

- Dark chocolate bar

- Chopped magic truffles

Preparation:

1. Melt a sizeable portion of the chocolate bar in the oven

2. Allow it to settle and cool. Make sure that the chocolate doesn't solidify

3. Add in magic chopped magic truffles and gently mix

4. Pour the mixture onto the mold

5. Place the mold in the fridge for it to solidify

6. Savor your psychedelic chocolate truffles at your convenience

Energy balls

Ingredients

- Finely chopped magic truffles

- Coconut flakes

- Rolled oats

- Ground flax seeds

- Raisins

- Cocoa powder

- Peanut butter

- Cinnamon powder

- Vanilla powder

Preparation:

1. Put all the ingredients in a big bowl

2. Mix the ingredients until uniformly textured

3. Roll balls out of the mixture and place them onto a tray

4. Place the balls into the fridge to harden

5. Serve your energy balls at your convenience.

PART V: HOW TO MAKE YOUR PSYLOCYBIN MUSHROOMS YOUR ETERNAL LIFESTYLE

ecstasy, joy, and happiness

Photo by Hensz /pixabay.com

Overview

Eternity is about having a moment that lives in perpetuity through indelible memories of an everlasting transformation.

In life, just as a beautiful landscape, there are highs and lows, twists, and turns. This is what brings up the beauty of life. Life would be miserable if it were flat and happiness like a plain. Happiness manifests in the highs after rising above the lows.

A psychedelic lifestyle does not erase the lows but simply raises the platform so that you can experience higher-highs.

While the psychedelic shrooms raise your platform, it is up to you to accentuate your high-highs through the right dosage and deliberate mind transformation such that you can actualize the psychedelic ideas and psychedelic dreams that abound when you are in that 'cloud 9' where ecstasy, joy and happiness bubble up your volcanic high-highs.

In this Part, we are going to learn how to take the right dose to keep your lifestyle platform raised and to rewire your brain, reset your mind and reprogram your mindset so that you can actualize your psychedelic ideas and live your psychedelic dreams in a new reality.

Topics covered

- How to use micro-dosing to inspire your daily experiences

- How to recharge your life, boost your joy, and experience more happiness through psychedelic lifestyle

- How to tap into the psychedelic power of shrooms to reset and reprogram your mindset

Chapter 12: How to Use Micro-dosing to Inspire Your Daily Experiences

Micro-dosing simply means to take doses in minute quantities so that you able to engage in a light conscious trip – a trip that does not bring forth a new reality but brings forth new experiences in the existing reality.

Why micro-dosing?

In micro-dosing, the purpose is not to take a trip to heaven but to bring heaven into your daily encounters. It is about adding value to your existing reality – work, focus, and productivity.

The following are some of the aims of micro-dosing:

- To have a safe psychedelic trip as a beginner

- To be in control of your daily activities even as you encounter the euphoric moment

Micro-dosing: focus vs. creativity

Do you want to be more focused, or do you want to be more creative?

Different levels of micro-dosing have a different effect on your mind. Also, this is accentuated by the strain of that you choose to extract your micro-dose. Dosing aside, certain strains tend to bring you an experience of mental acuity, while others tend to bring that experience of mental creativity.

Mental acuity increases your level of detail-acquisition. You can absorb more details from a given subject or object. This detail acquisition is a result of convergent thinking whereby different aspects and perspectives of the same object or subject converge to increase clarity, bring more understanding, and give rise to consensus.

On the other hand, mental creativity increases your ability to generate inspiring ideas. Through mental creativity, you can find different ideas of doing the same thing or different ideas of doing different things. Creativity is about diverging from the norm, from the obvious, and the common. Creativity is the outcome of divergent thinking.

While not scientifically proven, most of those who take psilocybin mushrooms in light micro-doses claim to experience improved mental focus. On the other hand, most of those who take heavier micro-doses claim to experience more creativity.

As a rule of thumb, if you want to experience greater mental acuity (focus), take a light dose. On the other hand, if you want to experience greater mental creativity, take a medium dose. If you want to experience hyper-creativity accompanied by complete euphoria and ecstasy, take a heavy dose. However, each individual has different tolerance levels. Again, each strain has a unique impact. Thus, the best way to establish your boundary between focus and creativity can only come through experimentation. Experiment taking different micro-doses and gauge the effect of each quantity of micro-dose on your brain. While carrying out this experiment, also experiment on the different strains/species and their respective impact on focus and creativity.

Nonetheless, generally, lighter micro-doses tend to improve mental acuity, while heavier micro-doses tend to boost mental creativity.

Micro-dosing: rational vs. emotional

Do you want to boost your rational intelligence (RQ), or do you want to boost your emotional intelligence (EQ)?

Generally, a lighter micro-dose promotes rational intelligence (RQ), while a heavier micro-dose promotes emotional connection (EQ).

RQ (Rational Quotient – a measure of rational intelligence) is best applied in the typical classroom/study/work environment. However, when it comes to real-life experience where social networking/relationship is more important, EQ

(Emotional Quotient – a measure of emotional intelligence) becomes of more significant importance.

Thus, take a lighter dose if you want to boost your productivity. But if you want to boost your social relationships, take a heavier dose.

Micro-dosing: Therapeutic vs recreational

Micro-dosing is generally for therapeutic purposes. At best, it is for productivity purposes. Micro-doses are too minute to have a recreational impact. Even though you can get therapeutic benefits from micro-doses, you can also gain more therapeutic benefits from recreational doses.

Micro-dosing: Truffles or Mushrooms?

Some prefer to micro-dose on truffles while others prefer to micro-dose on mushrooms. Probably, it is a matter of taste and preferences – for each psilonaut has his/her own flight experience. Nonetheless, when it comes to the general effect, there is hardly any difference between truffles and mushrooms.

However, if you are one who desires to store your potent magic for long, then truffles are not your friend. Mushrooms can retain potency for months while dry. But the same isn't the case with truffles. Most truffles diminish their potency as they dry. Truffles are highly perishable when compared to the mushrooms.

Which Psilocybin strain should I use for Micro-dosing?

When it comes to the choice of psilocybin strain to use, it is a matter of personal taste and preferences. However, certain strains appeal to beginners, while others appeal to experienced psilonauts. For example, Golden Teacher seems to favor beginners. PES Amazonian also does well for beginners. B+ isn't bad either.

As a beginner, Golden Teacher is the preferred way to introduce you to the psychedelic kindergarten. Afterward, you can take baby steps towards other strains and species as you gain more experience through experimentation.

Generally, when it comes to species, the following are the most popular species for micro-dosing:

- Psilocybe cubensis

- Psilocybe azurecens

- Psilocybe cyanescens

- Psilocybe semilanceata

- Panaeolus

Nonetheless, any psilocybe can be used for micro-dosing. What you need to factor is the potency of each species so that you can adjust the dosage measurement accordingly.

Finding the right micro-dose

As a rule of thumb, when it comes to finding the right micro-dose, start low, and gradually increase your dose. However, this rule is more applicable to experienced users than beginners.

Most beginners find it hard to notice the effect of a micro-dose. Thus, for beginners, it is preferable to start with a full dose to learn what it is to take the magic. Afterward, gradually reduce the dosage as the magic sticks. Continue reducing your dose for so long as there is still a magic effect. The lowest level at which you can still experience the magical impact of your shroom becomes your minimum threshold. If you take the path of starting on a full dose, have a trip-sitter to help you navigate the trip.

Micro-dosing schedule

The body always finds ways to adjust and get accustomed to your consumption. If it can't get accustomed to your new consumption habit, then, it will repel your habit.

Similarly, when you take micro-doses, the body tries to adjust and get accustomed to it. As such, it tries to bring normalcy – an old reality. This normalcy tends to nullify the good effect that you desire to get out of micro-dosing.

Thus, to continue enjoying the hyper-moments, you have to trick the body away from normalizing your consumption. How do you achieve this? The simplest way to do this is to avoid micro-dosing daily.

The best approach is to skip two days after taking your dose. For example, if you take your micro-dose on Monday, skip Tuesday and Wednesday so that you take the next micro-dose on Thursday. Tuesday (or the first skip day) is the observation day – a day you observe the impact of your micro-dose. Wednesday (or the second skip day) is the day you take a break from the dose. During the break day, the body has nearly gone to the level (base level) it was in before you took the micro-dose, and thus no longer feels the need to normalize the dosage. However, due to the effect of neuroplasticity on your brain caused by psilocin, the current base level could be higher than the previous base level. The long-term target is to keep on increasing this base level so that every new moment you get on the trip, you achieve a new high-highs.

Knowing that the psychedelic effect only lasts for 8 hours (time it to match with your working hours for maximum productivity), on the first skip-day, you will simply be riding on the left-over psychedelic waves. The second skip-day will have no noticeable waves to ride on. It is the day of sobriety. It the day of the 'lull before the next storm'.

I would recommend making the pattern very irregular so that the body has no chance of normalization and hence nullifying the psychedelic effect.

How to take your micro-dose

You can take your micro-dose in several ways. The following are the two most loved ways by psilonauts:

- Capsules – you can either buy ready-made psilocybe capsules, or you can simply pour your measured psilocybe powder into empty capsules, store them into a bottle, and take each capsule as needed.

- Honey beverage – if you like fluid dose, simply sprinkle your micro-dose into a cup of hot water. Add several drops of honey to boost your taste. Stir and then drink as a beverage. The advantage of honey is that it not only suppresses the bitter or unpleasant taste but also boosts the absorption rate of the micro-dose.

Chapter 13: How to Recharge Your Life, Boost your joy, and Experience More Happiness through Psychedelic Lifestyle

You can achieve a psychedelic lifestyle. You can be a constant psychedelic voyager.

You can recharge your life. Nature's secretly hidden recharge battery is now within your reach. All you need is to tap into its endless reserves. In Part II, we discussed how you can keep this battery within your reach and how you can ensure that this battery keeps the high voltage at all times.

The radiance of constant joy in this gloomy world is a rarity. Just as there are those days when the sun rises late and those days when the clouds overwhelm its rays, there are certainly those days when the gloom blankets your radiance. But, despite the gloom and the darkness, the sunshine never switches off. Its source of radiance remains constant. Similarly, I cannot promise you that your joy will shine all moments, but I can promise you that its source will never extinguish, for so long as the magic source remains supplied.

Happiness is not something to be pursued. Rather, happiness is something to be experienced. Just as you expose yourself to early sunrise so that your skin can experience that morning glow and its accompanying soothing warmth, you too can expose yourself to happiness. It takes effort. It is not that happiness doesn't exist. It is simply that very few know how to expose themselves to its rays.

Having a psychedelic lifestyle is the way to recharge your life, boost your joy, and experience more happiness.

So, what is this psychedelic lifestyle?

A psychedelic lifestyle is that lifestyle characterized by a constant trip to nirvana. Like every other long trip, there are moments to take a break and rest. There are moments to re-energize and moments to take a nap. This doesn't mean that the trip has ended, but still ongoing and still transitioning from one stage to another. You are still arriving!

A psychedelic lifestyle is a lifestyle that is constantly being recharged by the magic battery. You are constantly arriving. In this lifestyle, energy and vitality keep flowing from this magic battery into your gut, veins, and nerves. Your brain is constantly being nourished, and your mind constantly recharged.

How do I achieve this psychedelic lifestyle?

As I have said earlier, there will be a boom and gloom. And there will be breaks and rests. But, just as the sun never switches off despite the darkness, the psychedelic lifestyle doesn't end with momentary breaks. And like any other flow, there will be ups and downs. Energy is a flow. And this flow has its waves. You may have low-energy moments, and you may have high-energy moments. What would be the need for a magic battery if all moments were high moments?

Thus, achieving a psychedelic lifestyle means keeping your magic battery in constant supply and letting it keep optimal recharge level. Optimal means just sufficiently enough to maximize benefits – neither extremely high nor extremely low – for the extremity of both polarities have costs that supersede the benefits. You want a positive gain, not a negative loss.

Well, how do I keep on recharging?

There are six things that you must do (or rather, six steps that you must take):

1. Be open-minded

2. Set your vision

3. Keep a prepping routine

4. Keep a dosing routine

5. Take charge

6. Have faith

Be open-minded

To be open-minded is to be free to experience what comes by without attachment to a certain specific outcome. This does not necessarily mean that you have no hope for a certain experience. But, even with that hope, you don't set expectations. I hope for something but expect anything. I hope for a certain experience but expect any other outcome.

Why should you be open-minded?

The primary reason is that every psychedelic trip is unique. You can experience heaven – bliss, eternal joy, endless laughter, perma-smile, or perma-grin. Great ideas can flow in quick succession such that you see the philosopher in you sitting on top of the universe and providing all the solutions that the world needs. You too can experience hell – confusion, discomfort, terrifying ghostly images, panic, among others. What you experience is more often the reality mingled with the past mental images.

To be open-minded is to accept infinite possibilities. It is also to accept that any experience is possible. Thus, you set your mind free to experience whatever comes by without attaching your emotions to it.

Being open-minded is to free yourself from conditionalities. It is to stop forging or corrupting your new experience pre-birth with elements of your previous experience.

This may run contrary to my assertion of what you expect on your psychedelic trip. It may even seem to run contrary to my next assertion that you need to set vision/goals. However, this is further from what is.

In the open-mindedness, you are a constant traveler to unknown destinations. You are an adventurer. Though you've heard stories of someplace and what you ought to do to arrive there, and how the path to that destination is plus the experiences of other voyagers, you do not let these fix your destiny. You simply don't know the destination. Their stories and experiences are simply theirs, not yours. You are yet to experience.

Furthermore, in this psychedelic trip, you are not the driver, rather the passenger. You are not engaged in the mechanics that bring forth movement, but simply an observer. You are not crafting the path, but simply experiencing it. You have no control over the program that runs the shroom's spacecraft, but you have control over the program that runs your experience.

Set your vision

As I have said before, oftentimes, your state of mind before the psychedelic trip counts a lot in what you experience along that trip.

When you have more positive mental images than negative ones, you are more likely to experience a heavenly trip. But, if you have entertained a lot of negative mental images before the trip, then, you are more likely to encounter a hellish experience on your trip. Whichever the case, the good thing is that the experience temporary.

Setting your vision helps to flush out negative mental images. But this can only happen if you set up a positive vision.

Creative visualization is one great way to set up a positive vision. Through creative visualization, you can create positive mental images of your trip. Thus, as the psychedelic magic lifts you, the boundary between your reality and vision gets nullified as you slowly dive into your created vision. This way, you can avoid hell on your trip. The creative visions you have becomes the mental maps to your destiny.

Create a mastermind alliance

We exist because of others and for others. This is the reality that we have never fathomed deeply. The ego is a very small part of our existence. It is because of others that you were conceived. And it is because of others that you have learned a lot. And it is for others that you have a job, a profession, a trade, business, or whatever livelihood that you have pursued.

Similarly, your trip, if it got to be successful, depends on others. This is more important when it comes to psychedelic trip. You are a psilonaut. And like astronauts, you need a team for a successful take-off into your space exploration.

Create a mastermind alliance that will make it possible for you to successfully launch your spacecraft into nirvana.

Just as there is a need for a co-pilot, co-driver, etc., you need to have a trip-sitter. A trip-sitter will help you out on your journey.

Keep a prepping routine

Though the psychedelic trip lasts for a few hours, it can be a very long timeless mental journey. Sometimes, a few hours can look like years. Thus, you have to prepare yourself as you would do when you are going for a very long journey.

However, timelessness is not an experience for everyone. But, if you are new to this trip, you are not sure whether you will fall into timelessness or not. Thus, factor the timelessness into your trip.

How do you prepare yourself for the long trip?

The following are some of the ways by which you can be prepared for the long psychedelic trip:

1. *Have the right mindset*

We have already discussed being open-minded. That is the right mindset that you need to cultivate as your mental preparation.

2. *Have the right vision of your destiny*

Setting your vision is part of your preparation for this psychedelic trip. We've seen the importance of creative visualizations in your psychedelic endeavor.

3. Pack your belongings

What belongings do you need to have for your trip? Knowing that you are going to take a flight, it simply means that you must travel light – with only essentials. Don't cling – be it physically or mentally, to baggage that can only serve to burden and clutter your trip. Essentials include:

- Plenty of water

- Light food (such as energy drink, citric fruit, etc.)

4. Dress well

Yeah, when going for a long trip, especially as guests of honor, we dress exceptionally well. This is no exception when it comes to psychedelic trip. But don't forget that you are a psilonaut! Thus, there is a special requirement for your dressing.

Have a light, fairly loose dress. Don't wear a very tight dress that limits your flexibility and movement. Also, don't wear a very loose dress that can cause you to stumble. The dress should fit your body well.

Nonetheless, choose the color scheme that brings radiance. A color scheme that helps to set a positive spirit. Fairly bright but uncluttered colors are ideal.

5. *Eat well*

Eat well! This seems an irony. Why? Because the ideal eating for a light flight is to avoid being heavy. Furthermore, your tummy may not be such receptive to the shrooms. Thus, the safest way is to eat the shrooms on an empty stomach to avoid the clash of shrooms with the food that you've eaten.

But an empty stomach does not mean you eat when hungry. Simply eat some hours early so that by the time you take your trip, what you ate is already digested.

If you can practice Intermittent fasting with an 8-hour fasting window before your trip, that will be great. You can then match the fasting window with your trip. A 10-12 hour fasting window can be much better just to take care of the extremities of the psychedelic trip. With a 10-12 hour fasting window, you can begin the trip an hour or two into the fasting window and therefore end your trip an hour or two within the fasting window. This way, you are not disturbed by the pangs of hunger during your trip.

If you want to take advantage of Intermittent fasting during your trip, practice fasting at least a week before the start of your trips.

Keep a dosing routine

If your life has to remain magically recharged, keep dosing. We've already seen how to micro-dose yourself to stay euphoric.

The dose is the real charge material for your lifestyle battery.

Take charge

Whether you are piloting your spacecraft, or you are a passenger, or the spacecraft is simply on auto-mode, you still need to take charge.

No one else, but you are in charge of your experience. Your experience is unique to you. You may encounter the same circumstance with someone else, go through the same situation with the same person, but you will never have the same experience.

Your experience is not what happens to you but how you react to the happenings. Take charge of your experiences.

Have faith

Faith is not about believing or trusting. It is not about religion. It is simply setting yourself free from worries and expectations. Journeys have their risks. Accidents can occur.

But, as a psilonaut, these should not beset you. Your focus is on your destiny and the experiences that come along the way.

Faith is an attitude of mental, psychological, and spiritual freedom. In faith, you loosen out your attachment to expectations. In faith, you can declutter your path from the dirt of limiting beliefs, the vicious cycle of destructive habits, and unfounded fears.

How do I drive into eternity?

The best way to drive yourself into a psychedelic eternity is to practice a psychedelic lifestyle. In the psychedelic lifestyle, you are on an endless psychedelic trip. You are still arriving... and endlessly arriving.

As we have seen, on this endless trip, there are breaks, and rest – just like any other long journey. The most important thing to note is that even when the euphoric moment wanes, there is a long-term transformation of your state of mind. In this transformation, some occurrences are permanent – such as the psychedelic effect of neuroplasticity on your brain. The platform from which you take off rises to a new level with every new launch of your psychedelic shuttle.

For example, some form of neuroplasticity takes place. In this neuroplasticity, your brain gets permanently rewired. Once this rewiring takes place, it is bound to be permanent. Every time you get on the psychedelic trip, this rewiring gets reinforced.

While there is a big difference between being eternal and everlasting, to a certain degree, you can achieve both. Some form of your brain rewiring can be everlasting. Some kind of experience that you gain is eternal. It is not that these experiences are everlasting, but their impact is unforgettable. Eternity is more about being unforgettable than being everlasting.

Psychedelic retreat

One of the best ways to recharge your life and boost your energy level is to go for a psychedelic retreat. Psychedelic retreats are common these days. It is just a retreat-like any other, save for the fact that it is energized by the psilocybin.

Apart from tripping on the magic spacecraft as a psilonaut, you are in the company of fellow psilonauts and professional trip-sitters.

The location for psychedelic retreat is no ordinary site. It is carefully selected for your space launch. All potential hazards are removed. Safety is of utmost importance. First-Aid and emergency assistance are in top-gear.

While you can create your retreat location as you would do with a picnic, it is best to let the professionals do it for you. This is because they have the experience and are prepared to handle any kind of emergency that may arise should the spacecraft wobble or develop some mechanical problems.

Emotional connection

Emotions are vital energy waves in our bodies that enable us to communicate through feelings. The most powerful connection between people is an emotional connection. It is the emotional connection that creates the most enduring and lasting bond.

Unfortunately, in our modern lifestyle, emotions are washed away by the demands of our careers, professions, jobs, and etiquettes. We have been trained to mute our emotional expressions to appear 'professional'. Over time, through 'learned non-use', our emotional connectors become dysfunctional, ineffective, and even diminished.

Through the psychedelic trip, we can transcendent the 'petty decencies' of professional demeanor and reach out to one another in a more natural way, bereft of emotional connections, loneliness, and boredom creep in. These two dampens our moods and thus breed depression. Unchecked and unremedied, depression becomes a mental illness that ends up negatively affecting every facet of our life – and even terminate it. This is probably one of the reasons why psilocin has been found to 'miraculously' heal the 'treatment-resistant' depression.

To recharge your life, boost your joy, and experience more happiness in your life, you need to be emotionally connected with people. Get under the umbrella of psilocybin mushrooms, and you could find safety from the dilapidating rays of loneliness.

Social connection

We are social beings. As social beings, we can hardly exist without social connections. One of the leading causes of mental disorders is poor social connection. There is clear scientific evidence that there is a correlation between depression and physical disorders such as obesity. To a certain degree, depression can cause obesity. On the other hand, obesity can cause heart problems, diabetes, and other diseases. Thus, whatever increases your social connection boosts not just your mental health but also your physical health and overall health.

Psychedelic mushroom has been found to boost social connections not just among those who consume it but also between the consumers and non-consumers. This is primarily because psilocin is an ego buster. Selfish ego is what creates a wall between people. So, when this selfish ego is dissolved, then, an individual finds no reason whatsoever to buttress himself from those others who have no intent to cause harm.

Ego dissolution (ego buster)

As Buddha taught, our suffering is caused by our selfish desires. These selfish desires are triggered by a selfish ego. From a psychological perspective, the ego as a whole is not bad. It is out of ego that we can express our individuality and achieve our highest aspirations. However, when this individualism (id) goes against the welfare of others and even our very own welfare, then it becomes destructive. When ego dissolution is mentioned, it is not about killing the ego as a whole, but getting rid of that selfish individualism.

When the Self DIED

Have you ever encountered someone whose self has DIED?

Well, it is frightening to even think about it. However, Drug-Induced-Ego-Dissolution (DIED) is a great thing. Psilocybin is such a powerful drug when it comes to inducing ego dissolution.

When you board the psilocybin spacecraft, your selfish earthly being is left behind. You experience a new mystic angelic world where you see other beings as great beings to embrace in your mind and heart. Your social magnetism becomes more powerful as you seek to bring more people into your field of magnetic excitation.

Psychedelic Meditation

Meditation has been practiced for thousands of years. The same is the case with the consumption of psychedelic mushrooms. The common bond between meditation and psychedelic mushroom consumption is that both of them have been traditionally taken by ancient societies to achieve a desired spiritual state.

Before we can explore more on psychedelic meditation, let's first understand what meditation is, its benefits, and how to practice it.

What is meditation?

Meditation is the process of bringing yourself back to a state of being by which your self-awareness is optimized. When you meditate, you can stop following the maps that have been ingrained into your mindset to enable you to carry out daily routines. In meditation, you can reconnect with your inner being and reflect from within.

Like with those whose self has DIED, meditation detaches your being from the selfish, egoistic attachment to thoughts, concepts, perceptions, attitudes, beliefs, and even habits. You can watch them as they get washed by the gushing river that runs in your mind where such thoughts, concepts, perceptions, attitudes, and beliefs are merely an array of flotsam bubbles.

What if you get into that meditative state after the self has DIED? Unimaginable! Yet, this what means to be under the cover of a psychedelic umbrella.

What is psychedelic meditation?

Psychedelic meditation is the kind of meditation that precedes or is taken in tandem with the psychedelic trip – or even immediately after the psychedelic trip.

The purpose of meditation is to promote a pleasurable yet mindful experience before, during, or after the trip. On-trip psychedelic meditation is ideal when you are on a micro-dose. Otherwise, for a heavy dose, you either meditate before or after the trip. You can also meditate both before and after the heavy trip.

If you are new to the psychedelic world, it would be quite difficult to meditate while on your psychedelic trip. However, the best way to blend these two powerful mind-transforming techniques is to practice each separately till you are excellent in each. Once you become excellent in each, you can then start to gradually take steps to fuse them.

The benefits of psychedelic meditation

Meditation has been found to declutter your mind and thus bring forth clarity and a better perspective. This helps one to make more rational decisions that help to prevent pitfalls that perpetuate the vicious cycle of stress, anxiety, and depression.

In this regard, meditation acts as a coolant and pacifier. A coolant in the sense that it cools down the nerves, thus relieving stress. As a pacifier, meditation brings stillness of the mind, just as one would bring stillness of the water in a container to let sediments settle down for clean water to be drawn.

The magic in the shrooms crystalizes this cooling and pacification outcome from meditation and thus anchors the ensuing stillness to the ground. This creates a strong foundation for fortitude. In this regard, the shroom's magic acts as the catalyzing agent that compacts the solidification during the crystallization process.

With a clarity of mind, meditation helps to bring your mind to higher levels of concentration and focus. Higher concentration and focus boosts productivity as you can prevent the dissipation of energy towards unnecessary clutter. When your mind is decluttered, creativity is optimized. As a catalyst, a micro-dose of the magic shrooms intensifies this focus and optimizes productivity.

By relieving stress and depression, meditation helps to prevent or relieve mental conditions that are often triggered or aggravated by these two factors. Thus, meditation is therapeutic. We've also seen the power of magic shrooms as mental therapy. Blending meditation with the magic from shrooms brings up a more powerful dose against stress and depression.

Some of the therapeutic attributes of meditation include boosting immunity, prevention of premature aging, boosting libido, promoting reproductive health, and advancing overall sexuality. Furthermore, meditation helps to relieve pain sensations. The magic shrooms inject a dose of joy and ecstasy to this relief.

The psycho-spiritual aspect of meditation is that it boosts one's spirituality, releases held-up emotional energy, and thus getting rid of anger and grief. In this regard, meditation helps to boost your self-esteem, which results in greater self-acceptance and improved self-confidence. The entheogenic effect of magic shrooms advances this boost - in addition to making your grounded and free from attachments to a negative self-image that breeds fear.

When it comes to physiological health, meditation lowers your breathing rate and, with it, lowers your blood pressure, which is important in preventing or relieving hypertension.

Grounding yourself as a precursor to psychedelic meditation

Grounding yourself simply means putting your mind to rest. Most of the time, your mind is roving randomly like a kite in the air. In this roving process, it fumbles upon different currents of thoughts. And like following the direction of the wind, it flows along the direction of the most powerful thoughts, the most captivating thoughts, or simply the most traditional thoughts. These thoughts aren't necessarily the most transformative or the most creative. They are simply the most influential.

Putting your mind to rest is to bring it to consciousness. To see this roving for what it is. And to halt your mind's movement as an agent of the thought currents.

By grounding yourself, you can experience what is real: the real you that is free from perceptions, sensations, and emotions - A self that is free from cultures, traditions, beliefs, and knowledge.

Naturally, it is rather hard to ground yourself when these currents are still flowing. However, with psychedelic effects from the mushrooms, this settling down, this grounding, becomes magical. Psilocin acts like an agent that helps the various 'particles' of your mind hitherto dissipated by the powerful thought currents to consolidate and thus gain a critical mass to sink to the ground.

Thus, psilocin acts as a catalyst for your grounding, making it easy for you to quickly get grounded.

Meditation: how to get started

Meditation has no straight-cut formula. What is important is that you create that environment for meditation... and, more importantly, create that mindset for meditation.

A meditative mindset is one that is ready to detach. Detach from beliefs, myths, anxieties, worries, expectations, and such other kinds of psychological attachments. Thus, to cultivate that meditative mindset, switch off those mind buttons that complete the circuit to each of these attachments. This is akin to pressing the button to switch off the lighting.

A meditative environment is one that allows serenity to set it. Just as water requires to be still so that sediments settle down, your mind requires stillness for the mind clutters to settle down so that you can enjoy the mind's purity. To achieve this, make sure that your place for meditation is decluttered, clean, silent, and serene. If you are planning to sit or squat, then have a comfortable fabric to sit or squat on, such as carpet or mat.

Once you have set up the right meditative mindset and meditative environment, the next thing is to set up a meditative posture. A meditative posture is simply a posture that avoids physical stress and strain. When you experience physical stress and strain, that will ring in your mind and thus disrupt your meditative mindset. Getting seated in a comfortable posture that you have practiced long enough is the best option. In most oriental societies, sitting with legs crossed is often the best posture. However, you should not compel yourself to do such, if that doesn't make you comfortable.

After gaining the right posture, the next thing is to focus and concentrate. Focusing is a prerequisite to concentration. If you are a beginner, you can focus on a physical object in front of you. Let that object be still. Focusing on a mobile object or a shaking object can disrupt your concentration. You can also focus on the ground ahead or even a wall. What is important is that your point of focus is still uncluttered, and does not strain your posture.

Once you are focused, the next step is to focus your mind inwards. You can do this by observing your heartbeat or breathing rhythm. Gradually lower your pace of breathing while also increasing the depth and duration of your inhalation and exhalation. This serves to reduce your heart rate, lower your body activity/metabolism to the basal level. The main intention is to relax your body so that there is less pressure that causes stress or strain on the brain.

The final stage of this meditation is to switch the mind from being seized by the thought process. Free your mind from the thought pattern by not making a conscious effort to digest what the thought is about.

Continue your focus and concentration until you feel like stopping. When you feel like stopping, don't force yourself to prolong any further – unless you are just training your mind and body for endurance. Letting meditation end naturally just as sleep does is the best way.

If you can arrive at that state when you are no longer consciously aware of your thoughts, then that is the apex point of your meditation. It is like reaching the apex of Mt. Everest.

Make meditation your daily routine so that you perfect it with every new practice session.

Practicing psychedelic mindfulness

Mindfulness brings self-awareness while psilocin brings rootedness. By practicing mindfulness, you can disentangle yourself from the currents of your thought process. You set your mind free to root in the ground - to be anchored, so that chaotic thought currents do not lift you off during your trip.

Mindfulness is important in your trip as it helps you to develop that capacity to isolate the useful reality from phantasmagoria. This ability to distinguish the real experience of the trip from the delusions helps you to remain focused and thus overcome the dangerous currents that would easily seize you and rove you up to hell. Such currents include emotions, fears, anxieties, and worries.

Integrating your reality

Integration is simply about bringing different facets of your reality that had hitherto been forcefully disintegrated by the strong currents of distorted reality. It is the consolidation and crystallization of your pure reality – devoid of the impurities. Such impurities include toxic emotions, destructive thought patterns, rigid attachments, and selfish ego, among others.

In the psychedelic sphere, integration is about merging your trip experience with that experience gain from a mindful state of being grounded and then crafting a new lifestyle out of this merger. This lifestyle becomes a new state of being: a new being that is larger than the total of its constituent parts - A fusion.

In the process of integration, there is no predefined mapwork. The growth of the new being takes its course – just as the birth of a new mushroom. All you can do is to set the right conditions for the growth of this new being. Mindfulness, meditation, and positive experience from trip navigation become the critical ingredients of these right conditions.

Engendering an attitude of openness to new experience, being non-judgmental, and being attentive is the most important attitude to achieving a higher state of integration.

Devoting to your new paradigm of reality

Once you have achieved a state of integration, the next thing is to devote yourself to that new state of reality. You focus your attention on your new altar of self-awareness.

Why devotion? Don't forget that it is the nature of the mind to wander – for so long as thought currents keep flowing. It is also the nature of thought currents to keep flowing. In devotion, you keep your integrated being free from the effects of the flowing thought currents. To stop it from being a mere flotsam object susceptible to the chaotic bombardments of random thoughts.

Having faith in the source of your newly transformed lifestyle, having faith in this transformative agent, and having faith that every other trip will bring forth a new transformative experience is what it means to be devoted.

Cultivating a beginner's mind

Every psychedelic trip is new and unique. You may be an experienced driver, but that does not necessarily mean that you are experienced in all journeys that you are about to undertake, or you will ever undertake. Similarly, you may be an experienced psilonaut, but that does not mean every trip will be the same.

There is a lot to learn on every trip you make. To be a great psychedelic learner, you have reset your mind afresh. You have to vacate memories of the previous trips from it. You have to empty your mind so that an optimized psychedelic learning can take place.

Cultivating a beginner's mind is to always take every other trip as a fresh opportunity to experience newness. The old experience DIED on the old trip. The old lessons DIED with it too. You cannot vacate your skills as a psilonaut, but you can vacate your experiences. Your knowledge may be adulterated, but your skills are pure. Skills are a product of distilled experience.

Why cultivate a beginner's mind?

We've already seen why it is important to be open-minded. We've also discussed why meditation and mindfulness are important in advancing this open-mindedness.

A beginner's mindset allows tripping through an uncharted path. Without cultivating a beginner's mind, you are more likely to trip through the beaten path. Even though there will be some new experiences along a beaten path, a lot of experience will be stale.

How to engage in psychedelic Learning

In psychedelic learning, you take advantage of the psychedelic trip to veer off the beaten path so that you can create your novel path. You can hardly learn anything new in the beaten path – for all knowledge is the product of the beaten path. Knowledge is stale. Yet, the psychedelic experience is fresh.

Carrying out mindfulness meditation is a way to remove clutters of old knowledge from your mind as you expand the capacity of the emptied space to acquire new lessons. This is probably the reason why creative minds love micro-dosing as they carry out their creative endeavors.

In psychedelic learning, you adopt an attitude of openness. You detach yourself from preconceptions and other people's perspectives. What you learned before becomes immaterial to the new opportunities yet to unveil on the new trip. It is only through this attitude that opportunities for radical breakthroughs are optimized. Open-mindedness affords you the opportunity for deep learning. You don't engage in the routine of scratching the surface of knowledge through repetitions, regurgitations, and memorizations. You simply avoid assuming the posture of knowing and thus take every other trip and every other person you encounter along the trip as a potential teacher – someone with something to teach you.

Psychedelic relationships

Magic shrooms not only work their magic on your brain and mind but also work magic on your relationships. Your relationships get enhanced when you are on a psychedelic trip. This is because of the newly built emotional connections that allow recharged energy flows to reconnect with those of others.

From psilonauts own experiences, the following are some of the prosocial behaviors that they observed while on the trip:

- More connectedness

- Fewer ego conflicts

- Less anxiety, stress, and depression that tend to poison relationships

- Greater perspective one's role in the relationship

Psychedelic marriage recipe

An increasing number of marriage therapists are taking advantage of psychedelic retreats to heal marriage divisions and conflicts and thus forge a stronger bond between couples.

The following is a common psychedelic marriage recipe that you can use to create a stronger marriage bond with your partner:

- Set a romantic environment: declutter, dim lights, candle-lit psychedelic dinner,

- Take psychedelic dinner together (including a glass of red wine?)

- Have some few psychedelic bites while in bed.

- Have some psychedelic conversation

- Engage in psychedelic romance

- If set, have psychedelic sexual escapades

How to Share Your Psychedelic Vision and Ideas with the World

The world happens because of ideas.

A vision is simply that grander picture formed from pixels of ideas.

If the world has to change, then, new ideas and greater vision must come forth.

These ideas and visions do not come from supernatural beings, but human beings like you and me. Unfortunately, there are zillions of ideas that die because they were never shared. Visions turn dark because they were simply left to die stillborn.

We do the world a great disservice if we let our ideas perish and our visions abort. It is time to honor our ideas and enliven our visions.

With a micro-dose of magic shrooms and creative visualization, we can enliven our visions through the following 7 steps:

1. *Dream big*

We all dream. Everyone dreams. Yet, not all dreams are big enough to move the world. This calls for us to dream big.

To dream big is simply to create captivating dreams that can transform us, others, and the world.

It is not that there are only a few of us blessed with the ability to dream big. No. It is that only a few spare enough energies and put enough effort to create, nurture, and give life to their dreams.

Seize the oneirogenic power of psychedelic shrooms to dream big.

2. *Visualize your dream*

Dreams come and go. Unless you visualize them, they won't stick around.

To visualize a dream is to add imagery to it so that not only you but others too can be able to see it as you do, once you share it out.

Not until visualized, a big dream is simply a big idea. Visualizing it gives it a life form of its own. Making it have life means that it is not just a still picture but a motion being. It moves and captivates those who come into encounter with it. It is empowering, stimulating, and transformational. People can see that transformational potential. They can feel it. And can associate with it.

Tap into the power of psychedelic micro-dose to creatively visualize your dream.

3. *Cast your dream on a grander form*

Once you have visualized your dream, cast it on a grander form. Yes, use words that make it easily understood. Use words that make it highly captivating. Use words that make those you share it with feel that they instantly belong to it. Tap into the mystic power of magic shrooms to inspire people's emotional connection to your dream.

4. *Describe your dream's core elements*

The vision is like a forest on the horizon.

People can see how it perfectly covers the landscape. However, they cannot see the trunk, the branches, the leaves, the flowers, and, more importantly, the fruits.

Zoom your perspective so that you bring the forest closer to them in such a way that they can see the individual trees; their spirit can dance with the trembling leaves; their nostrils can partake of the nectar's sweet aroma, and their appetites can be drawn to the ripe fruits beckoning their harvest. Let the creative power of the mystic shrooms magnify the core elements of your vision.

5. *Package your dream in an appealing wrap*

If you have ever been a marketer or knows what marketing is all about, you cannot ignore the importance of packaging. Well, every grown-up adult of sound mind has at least once been a customer. Going to the shop where there are many new things on display, which item will attract you most? The most well packaged.

A vision also needs to be well packaged for it to be easily shared out.

The following are some of the features you need to incorporate in it for it to be appealing to those you desire to share with:

- It should be capable of being handled (short, clear, concise, understandable)

- It should be within reach (capable of being shared out)

- It should communicate a strong purpose

- It should be authentically compelling (being able to genuinely bring forth emotional attachment)

- It should subtly and covertly answer the question, "what is in it for me?"

- It should have utility (reach the right place, at the right time, in the right form)

On your psychedelic trip, draw from the well of creativity to bring forth that which quenches your audience's thirst for inspiration.

6. *Share out your dream*

It is not a great vision if it isn't sharable.

The worth of a vision rests in its ability to involve others. The following are some of the ways by which you can cause your vision to be shared out:

- Post it in mass media, especially social media

- Engage with recipients to create a positive relationship

- Form groups and communities of interests, each covering a specific area that needs to be implemented

- Rally people towards your vision – you can achieve this by using publicity, Public Relations, among others.

Leverage the power of emotional connectedness gained from the mystic shrooms to create a mastermind alliance towards your dream.

7. *Make it happen*

Actualize your vision. Enliven it by living it.

Begin to live as though you have already achieved your vision. It is not that every element of your vision will have been achieved. But, don't wait for everything to unravel. Start actualizing what can be actualized... and do update those you share your vision with.

Most importantly, know that actualization begins in the mind. Transform your mindset to align with your vision. Change your habits, attitude, and beliefs to align with your vision. Align your posture and behaviors with your vision.

Yes, let people feel that you are deeply in it. Only then can you begin to share with them the present of your vision.

Cast the new reality achieved on your visualized psychedelic trip onto your ground to guide your every step towards your goal. Let your steps be boldly assured in order to win the minds of the Doubting Thomas.

Chapter 14: How to Tap into the Psychedelic Power of Shrooms to Reset and Reprogram your Mindset

We've seen the power of psychedelic mushrooms in terms of reconnecting parts of your brains and transforming your mind. So far, we have not engaged in a deliberate exploration of the nature of the mind. However, it would be unjust to conclude this book without exploring the nature of the mind so that we gain an in-depth appreciation of the power of magic mushroom.

The mind is a complex subject to cover that requires an entire library of books on its own. However, we are going to explore the mind in very brief notes but without unduly sacrificing the need to understand the concepts. This way, we can be able to appreciate how the magic in the shrooms can facilitate the transformation of your mind to bring forth a new reality.

What is the mind?

This question elicits a lot of debate. It is one of those controversial areas where a clear-cut answer never comes forth. However, amidst the darkness, there is still a path. Some say that the mind is a part of the soul ("the soul's intelligence") while others say that the mind is a part of the heart ("the heart's intelligence"). Nonetheless, there is a common consensus that the mind is a part of the brain, and thus "brain's intelligence".

In this book, we pursue that common notion that the mind is a part of the brain. In this common notion, the mind is considered a functional part of the brain responsible for the memory of the past experiences, a set of instructions on how to detect the recurrence of that experience or similar experiences, and a set of instructions on what to do should it recur.

This set of instructions is what is commonly referred to as the mindset (how the mind is set to respond to various scenarios based on experience).

The best way to simplify our understanding of the mind's complexity is through analogies.

There are two analogies that best describes the mind's attributes – the Computer analogy, and the Library analogy.

The computer analogy – the best way to understand the programmable part of the mind

The best way to understand the nature of the mind is to compare it with the computer. In essence, the brain is a biochemical supercomputer. As such, the mind is a part of this computer. Our entire being is like a biochemical robot. So, just as a computer controls the rest of the robot body, does the brain controls the rest of our body.

We are now in the era of Artificial Intelligence and Machine Learning. One thing to learn from robots is that for a robot to work autonomously, there has to be sensors on different parts of its body – to sense the environment and respond appropriately based on the software instructions within the computer. We can equate these sensors to our nerves. All over our body are various nerves that sense the environment and feed the brain with data which it acts upon to instruct the body on what to do... based on the mindset. Thus, the mind is akin to the software part of a computer.

Just as a computer has both the hardware part and the software part, the brain has the "hardware" (the physical part) and software (the mind/mindset).

The physical part of the brain has a network of neurons (brain circuitry). This brain circuitry can be rewired through neuroplasticity. We've seen how psilocin works to rewire the brain circuitry through neuroplasticity. In this chapter, we will see how the mind/mindset can be reprogrammed through mindset reprogramming techniques.

The library analogy – the best way to understand our memory

Every library has a coding and tagging system to enable both librarians and readers to easily trace a book out of the thousands of books on the dozens of shelves. Without this coding and tagging system, it would be hard for the library to be organized and much harder for readers to get the books they need to read.

Every library has a register. This register has a record of all books. Within the register, each book has a title, author, publisher, volume, edition, etc. These are also represented in a unique book code. In addition to the unique book code, there is a location code that has information on the exact position where the book is located in the library. This location is indicated in terms of the shelf unit, shelf number, and the order number of the book within that particular shelf. In essence, this location code is the book's map. Thus, each book has a unique code, which is a combination of book code + location code.

Each book has a tag on it that displays its unique code. The reader can add more temporary codes to guide her while reading the book. These could include bookmarks, yellow tags, etc.

The purpose of the tag is to guide a reader to a particular memory (collection of information). A book is simply a collection of information. As such, it is physical memory.

Now, with this analogy, we can easily understand how our memory works. Our memory has registers, memory tags, memory labels (placed on the tags), mental maps (location maps), and mental images (mind books).

Also, our memory has a mindset that guides the action part of the brain on what mental image to fetch, where to fetch it from, how to fetch it, and what to do with it.

Our mind books are commonly known as mental images because they are more than the 'ordinary' books that we know.

For example, in a given instance of experience, a mental image will store such things as the sight of our experience, the smell of our experience, the taste of our experience, the actions and reactions of our experience, the environment of our experience, lessons learned, and a snippet of instructions of what to do should such an experience recur. These are more than what an 'ordinary' book can store.

We can compare this mental image to what we refer to in computers as an ISO image.

Yet, our mental image is much more than an ISO. It has data about the experience of our five senses concerning a given occurrence, how the brain reacted to this data, and future instructions of what to do when there is such recurrence.

The software analogy – the best way to understand our mindset

In this computer analogy, our mindset is software. This mindset interacts with various registers (memories) just as computer software interacts with various memory registers. The bulk of software comprises of stored procedures. Stored procedures are simply a stored set of instructions on what to do, step-by-step, should a given scenario recur. The stored procedures are automatically triggered by the occurrence of an event (as signaled). Only an external or counter intervention can stop this automatic mode from triggering or following the set pattern (mind map).

In this regard, we can consider the mind to be that part of the memory where the mindset exists. Oftentimes, mind and mindset are used interchangeably. However, this software analogy shows us that there is a difference between the two. The mind is a virtual container (or virtual memory) that holds the mindset. Sometimes the mindset is talked of as the 'programmable part of the mind'.

Types of mind

We can classify the mind either in 'storage form' or in the 'behavioral' form. In the 'storage' form, there are primarily three types of mind – Unconscious mind, subconscious mind, and the conscious mind.

In the 'behavioral' form, we do have a growth mindset and a fixed mindset. We have already seen what these two are in the previous chapters. We will still tackle them in greater depth later.

Why do we need to know these different types of minds?

Each of these minds plays a unique role. For example, the bulk of your permanent routine is etched in the unconscious mind. Semi-permanent routines such as those that you adopt for the sake of handling a short-term situation are registered in the subconscious mind. The conscious mind deals mainly with managing the execution of the routine as triggered within the unconscious or subconscious mind.

The programmable nature of the mind

As we have seen from both the computer and library analogies, the mind(mindset) is programmable. Thus, you can reprogram or rewire your mind. This is the greatest nature of the mind.

Like any program and like any rewiring, whenever the performance is not optimal, you can do fault-finding to search for short-circuiting - defects, and malware that make it not function optimally.

It will be rather unfortunate for us to continue with our discussion assuming perfect minds. This would be rather ideal than real. In reality, mind, as part of our brain, is not immune to disease just as our other parts of the body. As such, it is important to be able to know how to tell when our minds ail and thus cease to be optimally functional.

While we may not be able to dwell deep into each mind rewiring technique, it is important to mention these techniques for your further research.

Mindset reprogramming techniques

The following are some of the mind reprogramming techniques that you need to explore more about:

- Neuroplasticity

- Mindfulness Meditation

- Creative Visualization

- Neuro-Linguistic Programming (NLP)

- Positive Thinking

- Positive Affirmations

These techniques can leverage the power of psilocybin to deliver faster and more effective outcomes. Psilocybin helps to loosen attachment to the faulty mental maps that we have created out of our experiences. It achieves this by dissolving the old patterns of thought and behavior and thus opening up a unique opportunity for the mind to be reprogrammed.

Ancient religious gurus, while acting as trip-sitters and teachers, employed mindfulness meditation, creative visualizations, and positive affirmations to rewire the mind of their students (trippers) to achieve a renewed state of mind.

With the knowledge that you have already acquired in the previous chapters about the power of psilocybin in terms of resetting, rewiring, and rebooting the brain, you can easily see how these techniques work in tandem with the magic in the shrooms to achieve a faster, more efficient and highly effective mind reprogramming.

Resetting your mindset using Neuroplasticity

Neuroplasticity is the act of rewiring the brain to snap it out of the brain lock. Dr. Schwartz, a renowned neuroscientist, formulated the famous Four Ways process as a technique of dealing with brain lock.

The brain lock

Brain lock is a neural condition in which the brain is locked in an 'on' state. It is like pressing a bell button that remains stuck inside – there will be constant ringing even though you no longer want it to ring. Brain lock effect is best witnessed in patients suffering from OCD. In this condition, the victim repeats mundane tasks such as frequently going to wash hands, frequently going to check the door just to confirm that it is locked, etc.

In the brain lock, a given thought is locked 'on' such that it keeps on appearing recursively. The best remedy to deal with brain lock is neuroplasticity.

Psilocin as brain unlocker

What psilocin does is to unlock the brain. In the introductory chapters, we saw that psilocin rewires the brain neurons by reactivating dormant neurons, repairing damaged neurons, and creating new connections, thus enabling parts of the brains that were hitherto not communicating well to do so in an optimized way.

The Four Ways Process (4Rs)

The four-way as a method of rewiring the mind has been advocated by Dr. Schwartz. These four ways are:

- Relabel – Relabeling is about retraining your mind to distinguish between a real thought and a non-real thought so that you are capable of assigning labels to each class of thoughts. This way, you can ignore non-real thoughts and focus your energies on dealing with real thought.

- Reattribute – after relabeling, you recognize that the non-real thoughts are unnecessary noise distracting you from focusing your energies on the real thoughts. Thus, you can grant them an attribute 'unnecessary noise,' which allows you to easily filter them out of your thought processing.

- Refocus – once you have relabeled and reattributed your thoughts, you can concentrate and refocus your energies on what matters most – real thoughts. Whenever non-real thought comes up, you quickly refocus your attention away from it and towards the real thought.

- Revalue – in the revaluing process, you give value or essence to the real thought and deny value or essence to the non-real noisy thought. This revaluing involves assigning thought-processing energy to real thought while denying the same to non-real noisy thought.

These are the 4Rs, as advocated by Dr. Schwarz in his neuroplasticity approach. However, if you observe keenly at this 4-step process, you will realize that it is a more refined form that has picked some of the essential elements of mindfulness meditation and NLP. Indeed, NLP is just but a different attempt at neuroplasticity. Thus, these approaches – mindfulness meditation, NLP, Positive thinking, and 4Rs have a common bond and can greatly complement each other as techniques that can enable you to achieve a great result in resetting your mindset and, in effect, your subconscious mind.

The Four Ways Plus One

The Four Ways Plus One is simply the 4Rs we have discussed above plus one R (Re-create). To Re-create simply means re-creating or re-forming your inner being anew. In this way, you can create a new being based on the outcome of the Four Ways process that involves the 4Rs.

The learned non-use

One of Schwarz's prominent research findings was that the brain reorganizes itself depending on its usage. Thus, whenever there a part of your body, including the brain itself, which is not being put into use, the brain learns not to use it. It is excluded from the active mental circuitry system. A kind of short circuitry happens to exclude it. Your mind too can get accustomed to learned nonuse, whereby some of its power rests in the subconscious mind because you have not been utilizing it. For example, the power of intuition is such great. The so-called prophets, foreseers, are people who have learned to dig deeper into this mind power. You too have this potential, but, because you have not accustomed yourself to exploit that deeper intuition, you have not exploited this potential, and thus the mind has cultivated this learned nonuse. Psilocin reconnects the isolated neurons that had hitherto been disconnected due to non-use.

It is so natural that your conscious mind will always bring forth thoughts depended on their ability to be used. Those thoughts that cannot be frequently utilized will rest in the subconscious mind, while those who have no utility at all will be driven deeper into the unconscious mind whereby extreme energy will have to be expended to resuscitate them from that 'dead' status to an awoken status.

Learned non-use is quite obvious in our daily lives. You will find people who are extremely poor, yet they are overwhelmed by rich natural resources. They starve, yet they have extremely fertile lands. They go thirsty, yet there are rivers and four rainfall seasons. There are learned non-use of the rich resources available within their means. They have simply not utilized their intuitive power of imagination that rests within their subconscious mind.

Focused attention – the greatest tool of neuroplasticity

The subconscious mind is a mind in darkness. Without it being illuminated through focused attention, it remains in darkness. Yet, the power of this focus must continually become intense for you to dig deeper into and beyond the subconscious mind – the right to the depth of unconscious mind so that which rests 'buried' in the unconscious mind can be transformed into the potential in the subconscious mind and further transformed into kinetic in the conscious mind.

Taking a micro-dose of the magic shrooms can help intensify this focused attention.

The power of this focused attention does exist in the physical realms. Lenses are known to concentrate light power. When this light power is directed onto paper, the paper lights up and burns. LASER (Light Amplification by Stimulated Emission of Radiation) is such a widely used physics technology that emanates for the power of focused attention. The light is focused through a chemical liquid medium on a straight path and is bounced back by deflection of the prism wall. Every time the light passes and bounces back through the liquid prism, it gets more intense (amplified).

Laser light has been known to be used to cut hard metals like diamonds, performs incisions during surgery, and cut materials such a paper, metal sheets, fabrics into required sizes. Such power of focused attention! Just take your subconscious mind as this liquid prism through which of knowledge from your external world is focused through and acquires more energy from the properties of your subconscious mind such that more and more knowledge of intense quality comes forth – what a genius process! The light is energy. Your thoughts are quantum bits of vibrating energy. Light amplification, whether through lenses or prism, occurs due to the process of excitation or bombardment of phantoms within the light, which causes higher rates of vibrations and greater magnitude. Your thoughts too are energies that can be excited and amplified in the same way to get higher magnitude, which is simply power – yes, power of thinking!

Your subconscious mind is these lenses. Your subconscious mind is this laser prism. It has those properties that can excite your thought energy to higher states of vibration, thus releasing more power. It only requires your focused attention. A story is frequently told of Buddhist monks who can focus their attention on the glass until it shatters; on a spoon until it bends. Miracles? Yes, miracles, if you don't understand the power of focused attention. Yet, this property called 'miracle' rests deep within your subconscious mind and only require stimuli – redirecting your quality thoughts through it again and again so that it gains higher power. Studying is based on this simple concept. The more you read and reread a given content, the better understanding, and mastery of its concepts manifest. Why? Because the good thought keeps on being bounced back through the amplification medium – your subconscious mind, each time gaining higher energy levels.

Resetting your mindset through mindfulness meditation

We have already discussed mindfulness and meditation in Chapter 13. While there is a lot to discuss in as far as mindfulness meditation is concerned as a mind rewiring tool, this is beyond the scope of this book. For now, what we have discussed about psychedelic meditation is sufficient for our psychedelic exploration.

Resetting your mindset through creative visualization

Creative visualization is a cognitive process where one deliberately generates visual mental imagery for purposes of recreating or simulating visual perception to interrogate, enhance and transform those images with the intent of remapping associated mental tags or reprogramming associated interpretations to achieve and experience ensuing psychological, physiological, emotional or social benefits or effects.

Some of these beneficial effects include:

- Minimizing physical pain

- Healing wounds to the body

- Remedying psychological pain such as trauma, stress, anxiety, depression, sadness, and poor mood.

- Boosting self-confidence and self-esteem

- Improving coping mechanism in difficult social relations

Mental imagery – visual and non-visual

Through neuroplasticity (or simply reprogramming the brain), you are capable of creating different types of mental imagery distinct from visual imagery, thus recreating or simulating the intended experience of perception cutting across all sensory domains/modalities.

Some of these sensory modalities include:

- Olfactory imagery of smells

- Haptic imagery of touch (e.g., texture, pressure, temperature [hot, warm, cold, frozen, etc.])

- Auditory imagery of sounds

- Motor imagery of movements

- Gustatory imagery of tastes

Creative visualization is closely related to guided imagery in the sense that guided imagery is that part of creative visualization where an external party (a teacher) directs a student (the one carrying out creative visualization) to evoke and generate certain mental images that re-create or simulates sensory perception of either one or several specific sensory modalities.

In the entheogenic trip, the trip-sitter acts as the teacher while the tripper acts as the student. When shrooms are used for religious purposes, the priest becomes the teacher.

Stages of creative visualization

Stage 1: Image generation

At this stage, mental imagery is evoked or generated from memory, imagination (fantasy), or both.

Stage 2: Image Maintenance

 At this stage, deliberate effort is directed towards sustaining or maintaining generated imagery. Generated imagery is usually temporary unless deliberately sustained. Maintenance is important to ensure that the imagery process is transitioned to the next stage – inspection.

Stage 3: Image inspection

At this stage, the maintained image is inspected for clarity, explored for its various dimensions, and interpreted. This involves scanning the image in all its dimensions to derive its possible interpretations by the participant.

Stage 4: Image transformation

At this stage, the participant modifies, alters, or transforms the mental imagery through either remapping or reprogramming or both. Remapping involves recreating the image to a new image that suits a certain specific meaning. Reprogramming involves recreating the interpretation associated with particular mental imagery.

Resetting your mindset using NLP technique

NLP can help you achieve a better life in terms of your purifying your inner being, enhancing your personal development, healing, and developing your relationships and thus enable you to achieve a wholeness of wellbeing.

What is NLP?

You have probably heard of the miraculous three-letter acronym NLP! In case this is the first time you hear about it, I am going to explain it all right here before you.

NLP stands for Neuro-Linguistic Programming. As the name suggests NLP has three core components;

1. Neurology

2. Language

3. Programming

Neurology is a derivative of the word 'neuro'. The word 'neuro' comes from the Greek word 'neuron' which refers to nerve while the suffix 'logy' is a derivative of the Greek word 'logia' which simply means 'study of'. Therefore, we can say that neurology is the study of nerves. However, scientifically, neurology is designated as a medical practice that chiefly concerns itself with the diagnosis and treatment of all illnesses that are directly or indirectly associated with the central nervous system.

Language refers to the human system of communication that uses either, some, or all of the several modes of expression such as speaking, writing, or gesturing to express inner thoughts or emotions to make sense of abstract and complex thought. Language is important in enabling us to communicate with one another, satisfy our needs and desires, and establish and maintain our relationships, culture, and traditions.

Programming refers to the action and or process of setting up predetermined behavioral patterns.

Programming is indeed the miracle glue that binds Neuro with Linguistic. When it blends with Neuro-Linguistic, it gets a much bigger dimension transcending all the contaminants of the mind. It simply liberates the mind from its imprisonment by creating a map that establishes a path to the mind's freedom.

Having these basic definitions of the core terms sets us up to dissect what NLP is all about. ***NLP is the art and science that chiefly concerns itself with the study and understanding of how people organize their thought, feelings, communications, and behavior to derive their outcomes***.

In simple language, we can say that NLP helps us to dissect the relationship between how we think (neuro), how we communicate our thoughts (linguistic), and the patterns of our behavior and emotions (programs).

The fundamental concept of NLP

The fundamental concept of NLP is that people derive unique mental maps of their environment as an outcome of how they filter and perceive information captured through their five senses. In this regard, the word 'neuro' has a unique meaning and which refers to the mental map which is derived from an individual's unique mental filtering system for processing data captured by the five senses. This mental map could constitute elements such as smells, tastes, sounds, internal images, and awareness that forms out an individual's neurological filtering process. In NLP terminology, this mental map is commonly known as 'First Access'.

Just as neuro, linguistic has a unique meaning to NLP and simply refers to assigning personal meaning to information gathered from the environment. This linguistic process populates the Linguistic Map by assigning language to smells, tastes, sounds, feelings, and internal images, thus resulting in a heightened degree of conscious awareness. This Linguistic Map is the second map of NLP.

NLP is about creating mental maps. Indeed, any journey you embark on is about making footsteps along the carpet that your mind map unfolds right before your feet. You can never make a voluntary footstep without a mental map. Yes, you could be doing so subconsciously not to realize it, but so true it is.

The core fundamentals of NLP;

NLP revolves around these three fundamentals:

Subjectivity – each one of us sees the world in a different light.

Maps – our worlds are made of boundaries and territories that our life experiences draw out for us. A map is only a representation of a place and not the place itself.

Language – we have the power to redraw and expand those boundaries using mind manipulation systems, language being the most effective manipulator.

The core principles of NLP that you should keep in mind are:

- Other people's models of the world are not necessarily wrong

- The meaning of communication is the response it produces

- Everyone does the best they can with the resources available to them

- You are in control of your mind and hence your result

- People are not their behaviors and neither are they their relationships

Resetting your mindset through positive thinking

Positive thinking is a mental attitude that focuses on the better nature of being and visualizes the benefits that come from this nature.

The greatest secret of life is that no one was born to experience misery. No one was purposely born to live an unhappy life. We were all born to experience joy and happiness. However, due to some causes within or beyond our control, joy, happiness, and success have proven elusive due to the negativities that have shrouded our minds. Yet, in our mind rests the key to igniting optimism, success, and happiness. We only need to ignite this by starting positively.

To start positively is to look at your compass and find direction to where you ought to be. Only then can you make a move that is not an aimless wander. This too begins in the mind. You have to initiate a thought. This thought has to come from an understanding of its need to be. So, to start positively in positive thinking is to engage your mind to first understand what it is before giving it the right direction – a positive direction.

In this world full of competition, with success having been commoditized, sometimes you can feel overwhelmed if you can't fit the bill that is the price tag of this commoditized success. Success has become a product in the market whose value is determined by how much it fetches in monetary terms. This leaves many, whose success is not 'marketable' to feel frustrated and think negatively of themselves and, at times, about everything around them.

Positive thinking helps to bring out the original sense of success. A success that is not measurable by momentary gains. A success that is so unique that can't be put on a comparative and competitive scale of measure. It is in this original sense of success that we find our true nature – where we come to understand that we are uniquely and wonderfully created, and we have full potential inherent within us to achieve our unique purposes in life.

Positive thinking enables you to bring out the best in you, which you can share with the rest of humanity. Without optimism, the will to do this becomes overwhelming. Positive thinking invigorates your optimism, which boosts your will to explore and exploit your potential.

Positive thinking has immense benefits.

Appreciate the immense benefits of positive thinking

Studies continue to come up with the benefits of positive thinking. The following are some of the proven benefits of positive thinking;

- **Increased lifespan** – studies have shown that those people who engage in positive thinking have higher chances of living longer than those who engage in negative thinking.

- **Better coping ability to hardships, disasters, and distress** – Several studies have been carried out to establish how those who practice positive thinking fair on in difficult situations such as prisons, bereavement, natural disasters, wars, etc. compared to those who do not. These studies have found out that those people with positive thinking have a better coping mechanism for such situations, unlike those who don't practice positive thinking.

- **Lower rates of mental disorders** – people who practice positive thinking are less susceptible to stress, anxiety, depression, and other forms of mental disorders, unlike those who don't practice positive thinking.

- **Higher levels of immunity** – those who practice positive thinking have a higher level of immunity. This makes them less susceptible to conditions such as common cold and allergies.

- **Reduced risks of death due to cardiovascular disease** – several research findings have established that people who practice positive thinking have a lower risk of cardiovascular disease as opposed to those who don't.

- **Better wholesome wellbeing** – those who practice positive thinking are wholesomely better off than those who don't. Thus, they experience higher levels of satisfaction, joy, and happiness plus overall longevity.

Sometimes it is not easy to just assume that you can naturally stay positive. It needs the effort to achieve these. The following are some of the ways on how you can stay manage to stay positive:

- **Identify key areas that you need to make changes** – you have to critically observe your attitude, beliefs, and habits. Those that implant negative thoughts must be weeded out.

- **Check your wellbeing** – while your mind affects the rest of your body, your mind too can receive pressure from your body. Checking your overall wellbeing is important in achieving overall wellbeing. Check your diet, check your fitness and everyday activity to determine whether they help bring out the best of you or not. You have to avoid those things that don't help to bring out the best of you.

- **Be open to humor and laugher** – they say humor and laughter are the best medicine of the soul. A happy soul will naturally trigger a positive mind. Entertain yourself. Laugh often and much. Expose yourself to situations that make that come out naturally.

- **Live a healthy lifestyle** – a healthy lifestyle is a one that doesn't cause any part of your wellbeing to suffer or become diseased.

- **Surround yourself with positive people** – happiness radiates positive effects on others. If you surround yourself with positive people, you receive positive energies that boost your optimism and make you see things from a positive perspective.

- **Practice positive affirmation** – positive affirmation is one such great technique in which you seek to influence your mind through the power of feedback via your words. It reinforces the positive effect in your mind, thus helping to suppress and avoid negative thoughts from overwhelming you.

Resetting your mindset through Positive affirmations

Positive affirmations are positively-framed personal statements about who you are, as ought to be, in the moment of now. Thus, positive affirmations take the present tense since they are not framed about what you will be in the future but about who you are now as ought to be.

Positive affirmation simply follows the maxim 'what you think is what you become'. Thus, you seek to affirm the best of you, as ought to be, through the power of your words. This pushes your mind to focus on your words and deal with them rather than receding to the darkness of negativity.

Know why you need positive affirmations

Many people hardly comprehend how the mind works. The mind depends so much on the stored program that is deeply embedded in your memory. Your mind depends so much on this program (mindset) to interpret the present. This mindset (mental map) consists mostly of your past – your experiences, traditions, teachings, and even some subtle occurrences that happened in the past that you were not consciously aware of. Unfortunately, sometimes this program may contain negative codes (otherwise known as 'bugs' in a programming language) that may hinder your mind's productivity, thus constraining your potential.

To carry out positive affirmation is to erase these negative codes or kill the bugs so that you remain with a pristine program (mindset) that optimizes your potential. From this simple analogy, it is easy to deduce some of the reasons as to why you need positive affirmations. The following reasons easily come out:

1. To get rid of the defective mindset that limits your potential

2. To rewrite (re-code) your mindset so that you can fill the void left by the negative thoughts (bugs) with positive codes.

3. To keep testing your mindset, refining and reinforcing your positive thinking power

4. To provide no room (fissures) for negative thoughts (bugs) to creep in

5. To keep on activating your mindset (software) so that it can be dependable in running your tasks (body activities)

6. To achieve your highest aspirations – dreams and visions

7. To help others achieve their potential through compassion – sharing the rewards of positive thinking

CONCLUSION

Thank you for acquiring this book and reading it through to this point.

I hope the information provided in this book has enabled you to enjoy your psychedelic trip experiences. I also hope that through these great trip experiences, you have been inspired enough to start your magic garden to guarantee your supply of quality psychedelic shrooms.

Due to legal restrictions regarding the growing and consumption of psilocybin mushrooms, there isn't enough publicity about this nature's wonder-world hidden under the tiny umbrella of grounded shrooms. Many will be getting to know these magic mushrooms for the first time through this book. If you are that lucky, kudos! Nonetheless, some have already had the benefit of knowledge about these mushrooms well before acquiring this book. To all the readers, there is great value for you.

Why psilocybin mushrooms? The book has answered this question adequately. I hope you are satisfied with the brief information that could be pumped into this book. The answer to this fundamental question has covered the nature of psilocybin mushrooms, their therapeutic benefits, and why they are ideal for you.

If you have never been inspired to keep a garden in your home, well, this is the time. Magic mushroom is your source of this inspiration. In this book, I have informed you why you need to grow your psilocybin mushrooms, potential places to grow them in your home, and how to grow them so that you gain the highest potency possible.

Every gardener knows that harvesting time is the reward time. To optimize your reward – not just to reap the dividends of your sheer effort of investing in your garden - but also to cap your dividends with a bonus, I have shown you how to harvest your mushrooms. I have gone further to demonstrate to you how to cure and store your psilocybin mushrooms so that their potency is not lost to the vagaries of nature.

Harvesting is one part, but the joy of it all is when the rewards of your effort unveil to you a miraculous trip to paradise. All your effort amounts to naught if you cannot arrive at your destiny – psychedelic heaven. Even with great faith and best effort, without proper direction, you may end up going to the wrong destiny. You do not deserve a psychedelic hell due to a bad trip. This is why I have taken time to show you different ways to consume your psychedelic mushrooms so that you do not miss out on the entheogenic paradise. In this endeavor, I have unveiled to you the different methods of consuming the magic shrooms, how to take the right dose of your magic, and how to refuel your body so that you are sufficiently energized to complete your trip.

Last but not least, the psychedelic lifestyle is not about just one or a few trips. It is not about momentarily living in a psychedelic bubble and clinging to its walls till it bursts. Psychedelic lifestyle is about transforming your entire life so that you can actualize your psychedelic ideas and live your psychedelic dreams. It is big misery if you happen to go to heaven, and after its angelic enjoyment, you come back to hell. To avoid this misery, you need to engender a psychedelic lifestyle. A psychedelic lifestyle is about bringing that heavenly experience into this worldly reality so that you can transform it. And psychedelic lifestyle is about transforming your worldly being to be that of an almost omnipotent and omniscient being that you became while in the psychedelic paradise.

All in all, my ultimate intention is for you to live a psychedelic lifestyle.

Good Luck!